The Village Naturalist

by

Mark M. Peyton

DORRANCE
PUBLISHING CO
EST. 1920
PITTSBURGH. PENNSYLVANIA 15238

Dorrance Publishing Co
585 Alpha Drive
Pittsburgh, PA 15238
Visit our website at *www.dorrancebookstore.com*

ISBN: 978-1-4809-4623-1
eISBN: 978-1-4809-4600-2

INTRODUCTION

Every town has one. Here, in my town, I'm it. When kids find a dead bat, they bring it to me. I get the call about a strange snake found in the basement. I'm the guy who gets asked what that bright star in the sky every evening is. I'm the village naturalist. A naturalist is someone who studies nature; natural history; plants, animals, weather, geology, astronomy; in other words, a jack of all science trades.

In 1999, I was asked to write natural history articles for the *R.E.A. Nebraskan*. It was explained to me that the *Nebraskan* already had a natural history writer. However, this individual lived in Florida, and the articles he wrote were about plants and animals of Florida. They were interesting and informative; however, they were not of Nebraska. Thus, I was asked to write about the natural history of Nebraska.

Since my first article, one about toads, I have written pieces on a number of different topics. I've discussed a couple of plants (poison ivy and cottonwood trees); I've written about people involved in natural history activities; but mostly I write about various kinds of animals. These are creatures that someone in Nebraska will probably come into contact with sometime during their lives.

Some of those articles were published; many were not. About half of the essays in this book have been published; the other half are seeing print for the first time. These essays are about plants and animals that I find personally interesting with which I have had personal experiences. It is from that perspective, my experiences, that I approach each essay. Hopefully you will find these essays both entertaining and informative.

The Great Plains, in the middle of which Nebraska sits, has a wonderful diversity of wildlife, and it is a great place to live for someone with an interest in natural history. All one has to do is leave the house (in most cases) and go into the "out of doors," as my Dad used to call it, and they will experience contact with all kinds of plants and animals.

These experiences will teach more than any TV show designed to sensationalize Nature. They will also teach more than any essay I could possibly write. So why write them and why publish a small booklet full of them? Good question. I hope that my essays will not only teach you something, but also that they will convey to you my enjoyment and excitement about natural history, about the Great Plains, and about Nebraska. Possibly, you will then be motivated to go into the "out of doors" and experience these same wonderful things for yourself, and in the process, you will then learn something of nature and the natural history of where you live.

Chapter 1:

LICKIN' TOADS

Have you ever licked a toad? A strange question. Yet, one I've asked any number of school kids, Cub Scouts, and adults at presentations that I've given. A strange question to which I would expect a universal "No" as an answer. However, that may no longer be the case.

Me? Well, yes, I've sort of licked a toad, and for a long time I thought I was one of the few people around that would have that dubious honor. I mean, why would anyone lick a toad? I can't really think of a good reason.

If you have a dog and you have toads, you've seen the results. The dog will mouth the toad, and then quickly begin to foam at the mouth, possibly regurgitate the expensive special diet dog food you just purchased, and then, much to the dog's credit, it will never again "taste" a toad.

What happens? Toads and frogs secrete a fluid on their skin to protect against dehydration. They have special glands, much like our skin glands, that function in that capacity. The chemical they secrete also has a secondary function. It either tastes bad and/or is toxic. Thus, when a potential predator, like your young pup, puts a toad it its mouth, the results are such that the dog or cat, coyote or mink, may never again try and feed on a toad. This functions as a protective device for the toad, other members of its species, and members of other species that may appear similar.

However, that doesn't answer the question as to why humans, who are arguably more intelligent than puppies, would lick toads. It also doesn't answer the question of why they would lick one twice.

A toad native to the Southwestern U.S. has a particularly toxic skin secretion. Someone determined that a small amount of that secretion will cause hallucinogenic reactions much like LSD. I assume it was either a person who, on a bet, licked one of these toads and got quite high or a chemist who analyzed the content of the skin secretion and noticed a similarity to the components in other known hallucinogens. Whichever the case, the word spread, and the next thing you know, people were licking toads.

The toad I licked was that toad. I didn't do it on purpose, and I didn't get high. I got sick. I was on an extended field trip to the desert and was collecting and studying lizards, snakes, and toads. We went out one evening following a rain and collected about five different species of toads, including the lickin' toad. I put them in an old pillowcase. When I got back to camp all the toads in the case were dead except the lickin' ones. That's how toxic their skin secretions are.

Not only was their skin secretion toxic, there was a lot of it. A white material covered their skin and literally dripped off when I picked up the animal. I transferred the two live licken' toads to their own jar and preserved the other samples I had collected. Sometime during the process I inadvertently put my fingers in my mouth. A big mistake.

I remember a very bad taste and an uncontrollable reflex to get rid of that taste as quickly as possible. I also had in the back of my mind the sack full of dead toads that simply came in contact with this stuff while I had it in my mouth. I foamed at the mouth, regurgitated repeatedly, and as I said earlier, I didn't get high.

I thought back to my night in the desert, spitting toad taste from my mouth, because I just set up an aquarium for my son. An aquarium for housing toads.

Nebraska doesn't have a lot of different kinds of toads, only about five that I know of. One called the Great Plains Toad and another called the Plains Spade Foot are found throughout the state except for in the southeast corner. These toads may have been more common years ago because they live in pastures and grasslands, much of which has been broken up and put to corn and other row crops over the last century. They are well-adapted to the semi-arid conditions that characterize Nebraska. They stay buried until a thunderstorm occurs, and then they emerge, breed in the temporary ponds and pools created by the storm, feed, and re-bury themselves to wait out the dry period until the next storm.

The American Toad and the Narrow-Mouthed Toad are found along the bottomland flood plain of the Missouri River, and thus only those living in the east and southeastern portion of the state will be familiar with them.

The toad we have in the aquarium is called a Woodhouse's Toad. Woodhouse's Toads are found throughout the state and are by far our most common toad. They begin their breeding in May and continue into June. The males, who tend to be smaller than the females, sit around the pond and sing. The females are attracted to the "croaking" and seek out the males. The males will grasp the females and wrap their short little front arms around her belly in a position called amplexus. They hang on until the female lays eggs. Once the eggs are deposited in the water, the male then fertilizes them directly. The eggs hatch in a day or two.

The tadpoles spend about a month in the water and then emerge. Usually shortly after emergence, the ground around a breeding site will appear to move with all the small "nickel" toads hopping here and there. Once emerged, the toads feed voraciously and grow quickly, if they themselves don't get eaten.

Even though these 'hoppers have a bad-tasting skin, a lot of things do eat them: herons, snakes, and catfish. In fact, they make excellent catfish bait. But then, having tasted a toad and being familiar with the smell of catfish bait, that makes sense.

We have toads on the river, along the cornfield, in the irrigation ditch, and in the garden. My son has played with many a toad, but he never wanted to keep one before. This toad was different. This toad was attacked by the dog.

The skin-defense of the toad worked quite well, so while the dog went through its mouth foaming response and was losing the special lamb-meat dog food we feed it, my young son brought the toad in and asked if he could keep it.

It's tempting, as I write this, to reach into the aquarium, grab the toad, and give it a lick. Woodhouse's Toads' skin secretions, while unpleasant to the dog, are not as toxic as that of the lickin' toad. Unfortunately, I doubt a quick lick would do the trick. The skin secretions of Whoodhouse's Toads don't drip off the toad when you handle them and I would have to mouth the toad a while and let my saliva wash the material from the back of the toad and spread it across the various taste buds of my tongue. I don't think I'm curious enough for that, but then I would know what a Nebraska toad tastes like.

The small aquarium is finished, and I leave my son to watch his new "pet". The temptation to taste the toad has faded, and besides, I remind myself, I've already tasted a toad. Have you?

Chapter 2:

THE MARKER TREE

 I'm sitting in the shade of the old Marker Tree enjoying the cool breeze that makes it feel more spring-like than mid-July. I'm cooling down from my run. I've wanted to run on the Island since the first day I made the slow trek through the pastures on the two ruts we call the road. Now I've done it.

I drove out to check on the condition of the pasture and to do bird surveys. When I arrived at the tree, it was just before noon, so I changed into my running stuff and jogged back to the west. The pickup's odometer told me the tree was 2.6 miles from the dike gate. I ran to the gate and back: 5.2 miles. It was a good run.

I had a few minutes left of my lunch hour; so, as I sat back with my Gatorade and a turkey and Swiss croissant. I contemplated the tree spread before me.

I don't know how old the tree is, but Joe Jeffrey, owner of the property, told me it is the last of the five trees that were on the Island when his grandfather first came to this area. He says this ol' beast has been a big tree as long as he can remember. It's called the Marker Tree because surveyors used trees as benchmarks, and in 1868, when this area of Nebraska was first surveyed; this tree was one of those benchmarks.

At breast height, the tree has a circumference of about 20 feet, or a diameter of 78 inches. There is a general rule of thumb (and one that isn't very accurate) that for a cottonwood the age is twice the diameter at breast height... 156 years old!

That's old for a cottonwood, but not as old as the biggest, oldest cottonwood in Nebraska. That tree was located near Seward and had a circumference of 36' 9", a diameter of 139 inches. Not only was it the largest tree in Nebraska, but it was also the largest cottonwood in the United States. A National Champion Tree. If the "rule of thumb" is correct, then the Seward Tree may have been almost 300 years old! I use the past tense because in 2007 a storm took the tree down. The crown of "National Champion" for eastern cottonwoods then went to Kansas, but it's back. In 2013, a tree north of Beatrice, Nebraska took the title. It, too, measures 36'9". The Kansas tree is 35' in diameter.

To me, that is old, and for a deciduous tree, it is. The oldest deciduous tree in the world is a 400-year-old oak. The cone-bearing trees (conifers) tend to live a lot longer. The average mature sequoias are about 1,000 years old, and the oldest white bark pine and the oldest Douglas fir are 1,300 years old. Then you get into the real old ones. The Tule Tree in Mexico is 139 feet in diameter, and it is believed to be over 2,000 years old. The oldest known bristlecone pine (a tree of the western Rockies) is 4,900 years old (It was cut down to count its rings. Ironic, isn't it?). Some speculate that bristlecones may exist that are over 7,000 years old, and according to one Internet source there is a living sequoia (named the Eternal God Tree) that is estimated to be 12,000 years old.

However, those trees are elsewhere; not on the Great Plains; not in Nebraska. Nebraska is a prairie state, a place where grass is the dominant plant, and trees were typically few and far between, so few that Central City, Nebraska, was once known as Lone Tree because of a 50-foot tall cottonwood located on the river near there. That tree stood out on the plains, and the Historical Marker that commemorates the location states that pioneers could see the tree from up to 20 miles away. The Lone Tree was a mere 92 years old in 1865 when it gave way to a storm. Not only were trees rare in Nebraska in the 1800's, but native trees usually didn't live too long. The Marker Tree, the Lone Tree, and the Seward Tree are rare exceptions.

The Marker Tree, located south of Lexington turned 19 about the same time as the Plum Creek Massacre. Those doomed settlers could have seen the tree from their wagons if their attention had not otherwise been diverted. Who knows? Possibly one of the Sioux scouts may have been sitting in the shade of the tree when the wagon train was first noted. The tree had been standing 22 years when Nebraska became a state. It was 31 when Custer, on the Little Big Horn, met a fate similar to the Plum Creek folks. When the last shot was fired at Wounded Knee and the last person massacred, the Marker Tree was celebrating its 50th anniversary.

This island monolith turned 75 the year the 1st radio station in Nebraska began to broadcast and 100 the year my father returned home from Europe and World War II. On its 125th birthday, I entered college, and as the tree turned 150 years old, I took my job with the Central Nebraska Public Power and Irrigation District. A lot of history in that old tree.

Of course, the Seward Tree "saw" even more. This plains cottonwood had been in place for over 70 years when the Lone Tree first germinated and 75 years by the time the Declaration of Independence was signed. It was over 90 with the adoption of the Bill of Rights, and the tree's 100th birthday occurred about the time of the Louisiana Purchase and the start of Lewis and Clark's epic voyage up the Missouri.

At 150 years of age for the tree, Texas entered the Union as our largest state, and the seed that was to be the Marker Tree settled in the moist sand and took root on a bar in the middle of the Platte River. Shortly thereafter, the Civil War raged and President Lincoln signed the Emancipation Proclamation. A few years later, Lincoln was assassinated, the Lone Tree crashed to the ground in a storm, and Nebraska was accepted into the Union as the 37th State. At the same time the politicians were celebrating in Lincoln, Chief Turkey Leg, a Sioux, was cutting the telegraph lines and derailing a train west of Lexington. The Seward Tree was about 167 years old.

By the time the Seward Tree turned 200, it had lived through wars with Spain and the Sioux Indian Nations. By 250, we had experienced two world wars, the development of the automobile, and Rural Electrification. We also saw the addition of a state that was even larger than Texas. At 300, the tree had lived through all that we call United States History.

The Marker Tree saw half of that. Today, on the south side of the Marker Tree, there is a large scar. Inside this scar the tree is hollow. You can walk around the tree, knocking on its bark, and a hollow sound comes from the opening.

It's this hollowness that makes me doubt this tree will live to be the age of the Seward Tree. More likely, in the not too distant future, I will find this monument of wood and history lying across the road. To be honest, that was the real reason for planning my workday in such a way as to be here for my lunch break. Back in Gothenburg, a number of arbor monoliths fell this past week. Winds exceeding 80 mph came howling in from the northwest, and tons of wood went to the ground.

Large trees and small went down. Branches were broken and left lying atop expensive automobiles. Trunks were broken and twisted over the tops of houses. I don't know the loss in property, in terms of dollars, but the loss in property as measured by the shade cast by the many trees that now lie in the city tree-dump is immeasurable.

Maples led the list in trees lost. Maples planted over the past forty years, broken and twisted, were loaded onto trailers to be hauled away. Lindens, 30 years and older, broke as well and were lying across driveways, and at least one 55-year-old spruce fell, uprooting the yard in a 50' diameter circle. Someone planted the spruce, and then a half-century later, on a Tuesday night, it came down.

With the fall of the tree went a history of a hundred storms and the witness of at least a thousand lives—the lives of the people who planted the tree, sat it its shade, climbed its limbs, and decorated it at Christmas time, the lives of children who walked by on their way to school, hid behind it to surprise their friends, and collected small pieces of its branches for their tree books.

I don't know why history is so important to me and why the history I associate with these trees has value to me. I doubt the trees care. I care. Trees are special to me. Maybe it's because I've lived my entire life on the flat grass-covered plains of America where big, old trees are a rarity. Maybe it's a genetic thing linking me to the roots of my species in some rain forest in time. Whatever the reason, I do love trees and do hate to see them go down.

But, down they went; trees that saw the end of The Great War, the depression, and World War II; trees that saw the advent of irrigation here in the Valley and the changes in land use from pasture to wheat to sugar beets to corn and soybeans; trees that held strong through years of winter cold, springs of wet and softened ground and summers of drought and violent storms. Their leaves softened the blow of a hundred hailstorms and gave shade through numerous 90-degree days of summer's heat.

Fathers and brothers, mothers and daughters maneuvered mowers around them, sat in their shade with lemonade in hand, and raked the multitude of dead leaves in the fall. Then, from the northwest on an otherwise uneventful Tuesday evening, the force of air pushed by the differences in temperature and pressure over a large area caused their downfall, trees that now will never see the expanse of history three old cottonwoods here in Nebraska have known.

Chapter 3:

MOLES IN THE YARD

Years ago, while canoeing on the Niobrara River, I learned that some law enforcement people are never without their trusty "six shooters." It was the end of day number one of our three-day float. We found a nice little bench and were unloading the boats and setting up camp. I stepped on a rattlesnake.

The "buzztail" let loose with a rattle, and I jumped back. I yelled at the other guys telling them a rattlesnake was somewhere in the grass and to bring me my small camping shovel. Instead, the officer came running with his gun. Craters began appearing in the vicinity of my feet and I was dancing like a bar-room drunk in an old western movie. I would like to think that he-who-had-taken-an-oath–to-protect-and-serve quit shooting because of my dancing, screaming, and yelling. The truth is that he quit when he ran out of bullets. At that time, I took the shovel my friend Doug handed me, eased the grass aside, and for the first time we could see what turned out to be a three-foot-long prairie rattlesnake.

Using the shovel, I lifted the little reptile out of the grass, carried it up to camp, set it on a bucket lid, and thumped it in the head, killing it. The officer, reloaded gun in hand, bent over the bleeding snake and commented that he couldn't stand snakes. No kidding!

People many times overreact when faced with either things they have never seen before or are afraid of. I'm sure there are many things the police-man takes in stride each and every day on his job that would really spook me in the same way the snake spooked him. I worked with a fellow that would go almost catatonic if a spider came close to him, and my sister goes about half crazy when she comes upon moles. Yep, moles.

No, not the small clusters of brown skin cells that most people have somewhere on their body. (Did you know the average is 40 per adult person? I've never counted.) And no, it's not the traditional Mexican turkey sauce made from chocolate, chilies, sesame seeds, and other spices. And though it's the bane of many a freshman physical science student, this mole has nothing to do with the number Avogadro discovered as to how many atoms or molecules are in a specific mass of a material. (It happens to be 6.022×10^{23}.)

The moles that my sister hates are the small-insect eating, underground burrowing, almost blind, little mammals that occasionally show up in her yard, my yard, and just about everyone's yard.

She didn't know what to do with the first one that she found in her yard. It was a young mole and was out moving along the surface, looking to find a place to live. Not wanting the thing in her yard, my sister ran into the house and got a pair of tongs that she uses for special little tasks like removing dead mice from mousetraps. She picked up the mole and tossed it in her empty trash barrel.

That got the mole out of the yard, but trash pickup wasn't for six days. She could hear the mole trying to climb the sides. The constant scratching got old fast. She was also worried that once she started to throw trash into the barrel, the mole would be able to climb up on the trash and somehow get out of the barrel. She realized that to get rid of the thing it was going to have to be killed.

Becky doesn't own a gun and wasn't about to lift the mole out of the barrel so as to hit it with a shovel. She decided to drown it. She got the hose and filled the barrel about half full. It was then that she learned something about animals in general. Most can swim. The mole swam around and intensified its attempts to climb the sides of the barrel. More scratching.

Becky tried to endure it, thinking that it wouldn't last long. It lasted. She couldn't stand the scratching anymore, and she also realized she couldn't throw trash into the barrel with water in it. Reluctantly, she tipped the barrel over, freeing the hapless, half-drowned mole. When she returned with her hammer, the little bundle of wet fur was nowhere to be found.

I don't have the same problem as Becky. When I find a mole, I have three ways to do away with it: two dogs and a snake. The dogs eat moles, but they seem to have trouble digesting them and will regurgitate the darn things, usually right in front of the door. The bullsnake that lives in a large cage in the basement digests them just fine; she just has trouble catching them. The cage has a thick layer of sand in it, and the moles will crawl around and just about the time the snake gets ready to strike, the mole disappears under the sand. You can see it moving under the sand, but it sure confuses the snake.

Moles, along with shrews, belong to the order Insectivora. Moles are of the family Talpidae, and the one kind of mole we have here in Nebraska has the scientific name *Scalopus aquaticus*. *Scalopus* refers to a "digger," and *aquaticus* refers to the front legs that are situated such that the mole actually digs and crawls through the soil as if it was doing the breaststroke in the water. They can do so at an amazing rate, digging up to 18 feet per hour in loose, moist soils.

Moles are small, about 5–8 inches long with a tail that may be another inch. They weigh all of three or four ounces. Like most small animals, they have a high metabolism and eat their weight in worms, grubs, and other soil insects each day. That's one answer to Becky's problem as to how to get rid of the moles: get rid of the worms, grubs, and other insects in her yard. Some other ways are to set traps in commonly used tunnels and/or place some poison in the tunnels. If you don't like the traps and are leery of the poisons, you can try spraying castor oil all over the place.

Except when the young are heading out to make a life for themselves, or they get displaced, moles stay underground. They are most active during the early morning and late afternoon and evening. They do not hibernate and thus must feed year-around.

Moles are sometimes mistaken for gophers. Gophers are rodents with large, visible, yellow incisors. While moles are a pain because of their mounds and such in the yard, they don't really harm the plants. Gophers, on the other hand, not only leave mounds and tunnels, but they also cause damage to plant roots in the yard, garden, and field.

Moles are well adapted for their underground life. They have no external ears to get clogged with dirt. They do, however, hear quite well. They can pick up the vibrations of the air and dirt through their fur, whiskers, and the bones of their head. Their eyes are small, and some kinds of moles have folds of skin that lie over the eyes protecting them from the dirt.

Moles hunt mostly by sound and have an excellent sense of smell. Once they locate a tasty morsel, they crush it against the side of the tunnel with their strong front feet or partially bury it so that the prey can't escape. They then eat them at their leisure.

Most animal fur lies in one direction or another. The hair on my head tends to fall in one direction; the same is true of the hair on my dogs. But, that is not true for moles. Their fur is very soft and doesn't lay in any particular direction. Because it can lie flat any way you rub it, it offers no resistance regardless of the direction the mole is moving. The soft, thick fur from the European mole was once used for coats and jackets (the original moleskin). However, it really isn't a good material for clothing because the fur is so fine and soft that it wears out quickly.

Moles are one of the most antisocial animals in the entire world. If two moles come in contact with each other during any time of year other than during the breeding season, they will fight, at times to the death.

During March and April, if a male and female meet, they will tolerate each other long enough to mate. Come May, the female will give birth to 4–5 young. The young moles are born hairless and helpless but grow rapidly. About one month after birth, they are old enough to be independent. Thus, June is the time young moles are wandering around Becky's backyard. But I should pass on a fair warning to any and all of them. Becky learned a great deal from that first mole and has since decided a large hammer and a small thump to the head is sufficient to do away with unwanted little pests, be they a rattlesnake along the Niobrara or a mole in her backyard.

Chapter 4:

TRACKS AND TRAILS

My breath formed a miniature cloud preceding me in my jog, leaving a layer of frost on my mustache and the hair sticking out from under my stocking hat. Off to the north, in the un-grazed accretion ground along the river, deer stood with ears erect watching the dog and me make our way along the path that separated the cornfield to the south from this wet sand bog to the north.

Up ahead of me, over the river, a bald eagle flew with powerful, slow-motion wing beats. The eagle was headed down river toward its evening roost.

This is my favorite jogging spot. I had chosen a circular route that provided just a little under five miles of changing scenery. The first portion was along the gravel road with quail and pheasant exploding from the weed clumps that lined the edges. Then a stretch of field road that ran between what had been corn on the east and soy beans on the west.

At the end of the first mile, I was along the 96 Drain Ditch that provided everything from red-bellied snakes to great horned owls for my enjoyment. Mallards burst forth at almost every turn on this cold, wet January evening. Whenever I run this route, I count the species of animals I see. Usually that means birds as few mammals, reptiles, or amphibians are out and about during the day or at this time of the year. The lowest count I've had was seven, but usually there are about twenty different types of birds in the three habitat types I run by.

I followed the ditch until I arrive at this corner. Here I turned back toward the highway along the most scenic portion of the run. Here I saw the deer, the eagle, and the rabbit tracks.

I try to watch for tracks and other sign while running. On this day, there was an inch of new snow. Usually there are tracks in the snow from the trucks taking gravel from the pit located at the far end of the road. On this day, there were no parallel marks from the trucks as the pit is shut down for now. Instead, the snow was crisscrossed with a myriad of small animal tracks. I noted the different sizes of the rabbit tracks. I've seen both the cottontail, a true rabbit, and the black-tailed jackrabbit, a hare, along this road. Both apparently were in the area last night as their tracks were everywhere. Intermixed with the rabbit tracks were smaller tracks. They resembled the rabbit tracks but were too small. Mouse tracks. I have collected a number of different types of mice from this area.

Overlying the mouse and rabbit tracks were other signs: coyote and deer and of course those of a big brown dog named Angel (the Devil Dog). However one sign attracted my attention and told me a wonderful story.

Here and there throughout the tracks were areas where the snow was disturbed all the way to the gravel roadway below. On either side of the disturbance were short parallel lines in the snow. These were the marks of wings touching the snow, wings from great horned owls. Where these disturbances and wing marks were located, the tracks of some luckless mouse ended.

When I run, that usually takes highest priority, so I continued on the last mile or so to the pickup. The dog got in back, and I put on a dry coat. Even on the coldest run, I seem to be able to sweat. We drove back to the tracks, and I got out and walked around, reading the story of the snow.

One set of tracks was particularly interesting. The tracks zigged this way and zagged that way. Here was a disturbance area, but the tracks continued through it: a miss. Farther along the trail there was another disturbance area: another miss. Here you could see where the bird even took a couple of running steps. Farther yet there was a third area of snow showing the gravel below, and yet the tracks continued to the edge of the road and the heavy growth of grass beyond. This mouse had made it.

All in all, I counted six different places where a mouse had met its end, but there were at least thirty different tracks through the snow. What a party those mice must have had out in the corn.

Running is fun. Why do I do it? I like to tell people that it's like hitting your head with a hammer. It feels so good when you stop. I also enjoy the chance to think and imagine for an hour at the end of a long day, but lately the greatest gift I get from my runs are the different things like mouse tracks in the snow that I see. Yea, I could run in the gym or go up to the wellness center, and heck, we own a treadmill. I don't have to drive three miles to a place where I run five, but if I didn't, think of the twenty or so different types of birds, the deer, and the death of a mouse I would never know about. See you along the river.

Chapter 5:

COLLARED LIZARDS

Slowly, step by slow step, David moved closer, his arm stretched fully in front of him. In his hand were the two pieces of lath taped end to end. My bootlace hanging from the other end of the laths blew gently in the light breeze. Step. Pause. Step. Closer.

Crotaphytus collaris, all spruced up in his finest blue suit, sat there with head raised and cocked to one side. First eyeing David, then the string. Step. Pause.

Croaphytus collaris is Latin for the collared lizard, no doubt the "keeper of the keys" for this rocky ledge. University of Nebraska at Lincoln author and biologist Jon Janovy first introduced me to the idea of a "keeper of the keys." This was how he described an animal that was so characteristic of a place that the animal and the place become synonymous. To Janovy, the marsh wren was the "keeper of the keys" in the small marsh in front of the University of Nebraska Cedar Point Biological Station. The long-billed curlew kept the keys of the sandhill prairies north of there. Step. Pause.

I have thought of key-keepers in association with Jeffrey Lodge. The Lodge is an old office building converted to a place where 15 people can sleep. The Lodge overlooks Jeffrey Reservoir south of Brady. On the expanse of bluegrass in front of the Lodge is a mulberry tree. Every time we rent the Lodge, we sit in the shade of the tree, talking. As we talk, birds flock to the tree to eat the abundant fruit located above our heads. Inevitably, the birds are waxwings. Waxwings are the keepers of the Lodge keys. Another step.

On the prairie where David and I were working on this July weekend, the nighthawks hold the keys. I don't know if they can be said to be the "keepers of the keys" of this prairie or if they were just grouping up for their migration, but I have never seen so many nighthawks. Thus this prairie and nighthawks will always be one in my mind. Another pause by David.

On this small stock dam, or more precisely the rock ledge running around the pond, the "keeper of the keys" is *Crotaphytus collaris*, in my mind an animal that I will always associate with this place. Quiet now; *C. collaris* cocks his head the other direction.

Other lizards also inhabit the rocky ledge, as do a variety of snakes. Water snakes, milksnakes, and rattlesnakes are found in places like this. However, we weren't there for the snakes. It was too late in the year, too late in the day, though we did catch one water snake. We were at the ledge specifically for *C. collaris*. However, that didn't stop us from expending effort in catching *E. obsoletus*, the Great Plains skink, nor earlier in the day a couple of *P. cornutum*, the Texas horned "toad." Now, David!

David slowly let the loop in the end of the string lightly touch the rock in front of the lizard. He paused again. Then slowly he eased the loop closer to the lizard. Closer. Closer. We both held our breath. Now!

Now, David!

Collared lizards are fast. Very fast. They probably let us get close because they know they are fast. They don't know it like you and I know our street address or our names, but they know it. It's inborn, intuitive, instinctive. It is probably also somewhat experientially driven. Knowing how fast you are enables you to know when to scamper if someone or something gets too close. The faster you are, the closer you let things get before you abandon what you are doing and scamper away. My patience is running low. Not David's. He moves so slowly. Slowly the noose approaches the large male lizard.

If a collared lizard survives to adulthood, it is probable that it has experienced a few close calls, and those experiences, along with instinct, tell the lizard when the critical distance has been met and that it is time to run. Crawling on hands and knees, we had found that for most of the individuals encountered on this warm July morning, the critical distance was about four feet. The two laths taped together measured five feet. Thus we could stay far enough back and still catch the lizard.

With a quick upward movement David slipped the noose around the neck of the lizard. The loop in my boot string, our noose, tightened around the lizard. For the lizard, it was too late to realize that it wasn't David but the string that needed to be watched.

We transferred the lizard to the collecting bag. One lizard per bag. Collared lizards are not only fast, they are also aggressive. Fast, aggressive, and large. These are characteristics that college football coaches look for in recruits and apparently it works just as well for lizards.

Collared lizards are one of the most common lizards found in rocky prairies from the Baja Peninsula throughout Arizona, New Mexico, Texas, Okalahoma, Kansas, Missouri, and Arkansas. While collections have been made just a few miles south of the Nebraska/Kansas boarder, no *C. collaris* have yet been found in the Cornhusker State.

The males can easily be distinguished from the females. Lizards can change colors. The amount of light, their disposition, and whether they are in breeding season or not determines the hue of their skin. The large male David noosed was in regal blue with bright orange on the throat. He had been strutting around the top of the rock showing off for the brown-orange female sitting on the same rock.

Breeding season for this lizard is May and June. This was July. However, the male still strutted. Why? Who knows, maybe because he's a male and there is a female around. Males just naturally "strut their stuff" when a girl is around. Chances are that the females laid their eggs just recently. About 20 days after breeding, depending on the age and size of the female, she lays 2–20 eggs. She lays them in a burrow below a rock and then leaves. They sometimes do lay a second clutch, and maybe that was the reason for his color and strut. Sixty to ninety days after being laid, the eggs hatch. The young lizards are small and have banded markings quite unlike the adults.

Lizards are aggressive predators. Snakes will lie in ambush and surprise their prey. Lizards, specifically collared lizards, will give chase, sprinting and overpowering the hapless insect, small mammal, snake, or other lizard. They are the "king" of their little rock. Sitting out on the point of the rock, soaking up the sunshine, they remind me of the movie "The Lion King" with the lion looking out over his realm. They have that same "look" of power, of purpose, of relaxed confidence that they are indeed the King!

Like lions, the collared lizard is territorial. They will stake out a home rock, an area to hunt, and basking locations and defend them from other lizards. Other male lizards. If you know where a collared lizard has its "home," you can stop by every day just to say hello.

When you spook a collared lizard, it will do one of three things. It will dart away under a large rock or into a crevasse, and the chase is over. Or it will take off across the short grass or broken gravel area. After a few steps, it rises up on its back legs, and the "sprinter" of the lizard world will leave you quickly in the dust. Lastly, if you are in the right place, it will defend its rock even from you. It will puff its body up to look bigger than it is. It will open its mouth, which is ringed with a bunch of sharp little teeth. The back of the mouth is black, which makes it look even bigger. If you do grab the lizard, however, just remember that this isn't just an act. This lizard will bite!

David and I weren't on this Kansas prairie to hunt lizards. We were just having fun. Two grown men chasing lizards. Two professional biologists working on a different problem, a different animal, and for different reasons, yet here, after our day's work was completed, we stopped the truck, scavenged my boot laces to make nooses and were using electrician's tape to hook two pieces of survey lath together to make a lizard-catching device. We were taking turns noosing the critters. Why? I don't know. As I've said many times, when I was a boy I couldn't *not* catch lizards, snakes, turtles, and frogs, whatever. Now as an adult, an aging adult, I guess I still can't! We will look at the lizards, compare them, photograph them, maybe even sketch them, and then release them and move on. But for now it is time to catch lizards.

Now, it's my turn. Let's see if I can noose that female sitting on that reddish rock....slowly now...patience....David did it, so can I!

Chapter 6:

STINK BEETLES

As a biologist, I deal with a number of things that just downright stink. Whether it be the blood and guts of freshly dead or, at times, slightly putrefied creatures or the fumes from chemicals like formaldehyde, hydrogen sulfide, sulfuric acid—whatever, I know stink.

Even in my non-biologist life, I've run into things that were less than appetizing. For example, in helping people work cattle, it is not uncommon to be covered in cow…er…manure. My father-in-law, Dean, tells me the stuff tastes better than it smells. When people question that statement, he tells them that if you work cattle, sooner or later you'll get a mouth full of the stuff. If you're a "real" cowboy, you'll know the taste. Me, I've never claimed to be a cowboy, real or not, so while I've had it elsewhere, I've never had it in my mouth and will gladly take his word for the taste.

I've also had the dubious pleasure of having human…er…manure on me. In college, I worked as a bartender. A great job! On my first night, Dub was teaching me everything I needed to know to be a bartender when one of the patrons, who had been in the bar a little too long, headed for the restroom. We waited. The guy was in there a long time. Upon coming out, Dub grabbed my arm and said, "Come on."

We went in, and sure enough the toilet was a mess and the entire room smelled of, well, you know. Dub flushed the toilet and handed me a rag. "Clean that up," he said. "I want my bathrooms to be the cleanest in town." When I hesitated, he said, "Oh, clean it up. It won't go through skin. You can wash it off!"

Dub was a big man, and at the time, he was the only Chadron State graduate to ever play professional football. I didn't argue with him about just how many things "out there" could go directly through my skin. I gritted my teeth and plunged in with the rag. I don't know if anything in that water went through the epidermis of my hands, but I promise you, I just about washed that layer of skin clear off!

As ugly as a mouth full of manure or my hands in a filthy toilet are, the ugliest smell I've ever encountered came from a beetle. No, not a bombardier beetle or stink "bug," but a burying beetle. An American Burying Beetle to be exact, though other kinds also stink.

I was pit-fall trapping for shrews in the Platte Valley and had to close up the traps for a while. Somehow between closing the traps and re-opening them a month later the lid on one had been either taken off or knocked off and it had rained. A couple of mice and a shrew or two had fallen into the trap and drowned. The smell of their rotting bodies had attracted carrion beetles, including burying beetles. The beetles got into the trap, couldn't get out, drowned in the water in the bottom, and their dead bodies attracted even more beetles.

When I finally got to the trap, mixed in the "soup" in the bottom of the five-gallon bucket were about 300 individual beetles comprising a dozen or so different species. Three of the beetles were of the species *Nicrophorus americanus*, otherwise known as the American Burying Beetle. Why is that important? Because the American Burying Beetle is on the Endangered Species List. Oh boy, was I in trouble.

I picked the beetles out of that mess and took them back to the office. As I walked by Deb, our secretary, she gave me a squinty-eyed look and wrinkled her nose. I put the beetles on my desk and went in to wash my hands. I got back and contacted the State Museum in Lincoln. I wanted verification that these were in fact American Burying Beetles before I broke the bad news to my boss that I had found yet another endangered species along the Platte.

The museum wanted me to send the beetles to them, so after washing my hands a second time, I went home to get a container. I told my wife about my adventure and went back to the office. I put the dead insects in alcohol and shipped them to Lincoln. I then went in and washed my hands a third time. My office mate, Ted, told me to never bring those stinkin' blankety-blank things into the office again. When I went home for lunch, my wife told me to get those stinking blankety-blank things out of her house. I explained they were never in the house, and she explained that she could smell them. What she smelled were my hands, so I washed them a fourth time.

What made these beetles smell so bad was not just that they were dead. Nor was it that burying beetles eat dead, rotten, smelly stuff which they digest and then their waste products smell even worse. No, like a skunk, the beetle, if disturbed or threatened, can take some of that waste product and mix it with other fluids and release an absolutely nauseating stream of liquid stench. Apparently the three in the bucket had done so.

However, that stench is only one of their amazing secretions. Strangely, they have another secretion that does exactly the opposite of the one that smells so bad.

As I said earlier, they are attracted to the smell of dead flesh, sometimes from as far away as two miles. They fly to the dead animal and investigate. So do a zillion other creatures. Here in Nebraska, 10 of those creatures are other species of burying beetles, so the first thing the American Burying Beetle must do is chase all the other species away. That's not hard because the American-type beetle is the biggest. Then they turn against each other. The males form an arena and do battle while at the same time the females "duke" it out. When the dust clears, there is one male and one female left. The two then crawl under the dead animal, roll over on their backs, and "bench press" the critter.

In order to survive, these beetles need an animal large enough to provide food for the two adults and the babies and yet small enough to bury. A prairie dog or pocket gopher is about the right size, as are turkey and pheasant chicks. If it is too big to lift, then it is too big to bury. They will feed on it, say "good-bye" to each other, and fly off in search of another dead animal and start the entire process over again.

If the animal is small enough to bury, they do so. Like little bulldozers, they push the dirt out from under the animal so that it sinks slowly into the hole. Once the hole is deep enough, they crawl out from under the animal and start pushing the dirt back over the top.

Once buried, the animal is now out of sight of other scavengers like crows and magpies. However, it still stinks. The two beetles bite off the fur or feathers and completely skin the animal. They then roll the carcass into a ball and start secreting a second fluid. This fluid is a gray material that, once on the animal, completely cancels out any smell. Biologists have hypothesized that this material kills the bacteria that causes decay, and thus the smell of death. I mentioned this once at a symposium in a talk I gave about these beetles. Some students from the University of Nebraska-Kearney decided to test that hypothesis. These students took some of the gray-goo from a different species of burying beetle (because the American Burying Beetle is rare) and put it on Petri dishes containing various bacteria cultures. The goo killed the bacteria. Thus, it looks like the hypothesis that this goo controls the smell by killing bacteria just might be correct.

Once the goo is on the animal, it now is "out of smell" of scavengers like coyote and skunk. The next step is to mate, lay eggs, and then, unlike other insects, hang around and raise the "kids." Also unlike other insects, there are only 5-10 kids, not thousands. Unlike other insects, the male hangs around and helps the female. Finally, unlike most other insects, upon hatching, the grubs are so small that they can't feed themselves, so the parents eat the meat, digest it, and then like a coyote or robin, they regurgitate it for the young-ins'. Some biologists have even described "begging" of the adults for food by the grubs.

It takes the young grubs about two weeks or so to mature, crawl off, and pupate. The parents then leave, live out the remainder of the summer, and die that fall. The young beetles emerge and feed, find a place to hibernate, and lay over for next spring.

The first revoltingly smelly secretion protects the beetles from other carrion eaters that might also be drawn to the dead animal. One whiff of that stuff may even turn a coyote's stomach. The second secretion protects the grub's food so that it doesn't rot and isn't dug up during the two to three weeks they are actively feeding on it. I only wish I had gotten that second secretion on me and not the first. You know, if I try, I think I can still catch a faint wisp of that odor on my hands, because Dub, this, eh…stuff didn't wash off!

Chapter 7:
FUNGUS

Among my many faults is an almost uncontrollable fondness for food, something that, along with my advance into middle age, has resulted in a corresponding advance in waist size.

Having been born in Wyoming and reared in Nebraska, I'm addicted to beef, am always welcome to the idea of a pork roast, enjoy turkey, ham, and of course my mother-in-law's award-winning fried chicken. Throw in some onions, potatoes, tomatoes, broccoli, and green beans, and I have just about all the food groups covered. But there are limits.

I don't eat cow brain or tongue. I just don't. I don't like liver. I stay away from raw fish, and, of course, mushrooms are completely out of the question. All my life people have tried to get me to eat mushrooms. My mother and my wife use cream of mushroom soup for just about every sauce imaginable. When we go to fancy restaurants, they cover my perfectly good steak with the darn things. Here at home, Cindy and the boys insist on having them on pizza.

Why don't I like mushrooms? Well, first, I really don't care for their flavor. Second, when I bite into them, the texture is enough to stimulate my gag reflex, and third, hey, they're a fungus!

Fungi are that group of living things that aren't really plants, and they sure aren't animals. They…every darn one of them…live as parasites or decomposers on living or once living tissues. Okay! Maybe not every one. There are those that are symbiotic with the roots of plants and as such, necessary in the lives of the plants, but usually when we think of fungus, it's the parasites and saprophytes we have in mind.

The body of the mushroom, or any fungus for that matter, is typically an interwoven mat of microscopic strands or threads called a mycelium. When you eat a mushroom, it's not this body that is eaten. The part eaten is the reproductive organ! Now, I like "mountain oysters" as well as the next person, but the thought of eating the reproductive organs of a fungus…well, that's reason number four not to.

There are four basic types of fungus. All look pretty much the same, except for their reproductive organs. The "tube fungi" have swellings called sporangia that are located at the end of tubes or filaments, which stand above the surface upon which the fungus lives. Inside these sporangia are thousands of spores that are the "seeds" of the fungus. The best example of tube fungus is black bread mold. Other examples are downy mildew, which was responsible for the potato blight of Ireland in the 1800's, water molds, and a variety of rusts that plague our gardens.

The "club fungi" are the mushrooms and relatives like wheat rust, corn smut, and puff balls. Club fungi typically form the large umbrella or club-shaped reproductive organ that we call a mushroom. The cap of this club protects a series of folded spore containing tissues called the "gills." This structure grows quickly, usually overnight. The cap pushes its way up through the soil and into the air. The cap then opens, exposing the gills on the underside to the air. The spores are released to fly everywhere, and the stalk and cap dry and begin to decompose. Usually the entire process only takes a couple of days or so.

Many different kinds of mushrooms are collected and eaten by people, and many contain chemicals that are quite poisonous—reason number five to leave them alone! The poisonous mushrooms are sometimes called toadstools. (The differences between the poisonous and non-poisonous species can be so slight that only the most accomplished expert in the field can separate them, hence, mushroom collecting can be a very dangerous thing to do. When in doubt, don't.)

The "sac fungi" are things like *Penicillium*, one species of which Sir Alexander Fleming discovered killed bacteria. This gave rise to the entire group of medicines we call antibiotics. Other examples are *Aspergillus*, often found on leather and citrus fruits, and then there are the mildews, truffles, and morels. This group includes the molds that create Roquefort and "blue cheese" and other favorites. They produce small sacs of spores on specialized stalks. The sac fungi are related to the many unicellular fungi like yeast.

Lastly is what we call the "imperfect fungi." They are "imperfect" only because, to date, we haven't figured out how, or if, they sexually reproduce. Most of these are related to either the sac or club fungus, and examples include the fungi that cause ringworm, athlete's foot, and jock itch.

An individual fungus starts out as a spore. The spore grows into a filament called a hypha, which then grows and branches out to form a mat of filaments, or the mycelium.

Because fungi do not produce their own food, they must "eat." They do this by secreting digestive fluids from the many hyphae. These digestive fluids are harmless to the hyphae but are able to break down the surrounding material into a liquid, which the hyphae then soak up.

This digestive process results not only in the loss of material, bread in the case of bread mold, leather and fruit in the case of *Aspergillus*, and your skin with ringworm, but the chemicals released are responsible for the "flavoring" of the material by the mold. This "flavoring" can be a negative thing, as in moldy bread, or a positive thing, like the flavoring of blue cheese.

Fungi are relatively easy to grow, either on some old cheese, damp bread, or in a Petri dish. You can leave the material out to collect spores. Then you just have to keep the material moist, and in no time, you have a fungus culture. In fact, researchers from the University of Nebraska at Lincoln inventoried the kinds of fungi that exist in the mature forests of the Platte River. They did this so as to evaluate the impact of various management activities on this community of living things. To do this, interestingly enough, they put out "bait" to attract the fungus. That bait consists of cloth disks soaked in sugar water. These are placed in the forest and allowed to "collect" fungus spores. The spores start to grow, and the disks can be returned to the lab where the fungus is cultivated until it reaches the reproductive stage, at which time it can be identified.

As interesting as that is, however, that's not what got me to thinking about fungus and writing about mushrooms. The impetus for that has been an unusually bountiful year for morels. They are everywhere, and for the first time in my life I collected some and brought them home to eat.

Morels are sometimes called truffles, but they are not true truffles. Truffles live totally underground on the rotting roots of trees. Morels are also called mushrooms, but they are not mushrooms. As stated earlier, morels are sac fungi related to *Penicillium* while mushrooms are club fungi related, in a roundabout way, to jock itch. I decided that while I could never bring myself to collect and eat the cousins to jock itch, I could bring myself to eat something related to a fungus that kills bacteria.

Actually, morels make a good choice of fungus to collect and eat. They are very easy to identify. They have a hollow stalk and a spongy, pitted head that doesn't look at all like the cap of a mushroom. There is one morel look-alike that is dangerous, however. It has a short, rounded head and is darker coffee-brown in color.

Morels are found all along the river in the sandy soils underlying the river-bank forest. The actual body of the morel is underground, feeding on rotting wood. When the temperature and moisture are just right, the fungus produces the ascocarp, which pushes its way up through the sand to the surface. There it matures, releases spores from the asci, or spore sacs, dries, and decays. This is the structure that I went looking for. This year, they were not hard to find, and soon, literally within 10 minutes, I had enough for three meals.

Cooking them, it turns out, is as simple and easy as collecting them. One way of cooking them is to sauté them on the stove in butter or oil. We went the more complicated route, however. Sautéed morels would be too much like sautéed mushrooms in my mind, so instead I rolled them in batter and corn flake crumbs and then deep fat fried them. I do have to admit, they were tasty; however, the truth is that with enough batter, just about anything tastes good… even the reproductive organs of a rotten-wood-eating fungus.

Chapter 8:
RACING SNAKES

With the end of winter and the warm days and nights of late spring, I usually get to thinking about snakes and such. I've always liked snakes and have kept them as pets, given programs about them, and written a poster for the University State Museum about them.

Of course, once I start thinking about snakes, it's not long before I have a couple of aquariums outfitted with a bull snake or two, hognose snakes, garter snakes, or a racer. So it was on that day last summer when my mother-in-law came to visit.

The boys are always excited when Grandma comes to visit and are anxious to share with her anything different from the last visit. That was true on that summer Monday morning. Cindy, her mother, and a friend of her mother's were enjoying a cup of coffee out on the porch in the cool of the morning. The boys went to the dog pen, where the snake cages are kept during the warmer months, and brought out a small hognose snake to show the ladies.

Though the boys didn't know it at the time, they learned very quickly that both Grandma and her friend not only hated snakes, but also they were very, very afraid of them. Chairs were overturned and screams emitted. That coupled with their mother's scolding combined to excite the dog, who came out from under the table with her tailing beating back and forth and the "let's play" look in her eye. Startled by the response of the two guests, and bumped by the dog, the snake was accidentally dropped on the floor by a surprised little boy. The level of excitement rose another notch. The ladies were fighting the screen door to get inside, Cindy was trying to help catch the thing, and Alex was fighting the dog to keep her from making a quick meal of the small snake.

All's well that ends well. The snake adventure ended with the small reptile being returned safely to its temporary cage and the boys apologizing to the guests. Later, when Grandma and Cindy related the story to me it naturally led to a discussion of one of the two things my mother-in-law and I disagree on.

The first thing my mother-in-law and I disagree on is wasting a perfectly good homemade piecrust by using it on a green tomato pie—a pie that fools some poor devil (me) into thinking he is having apple pie for dinner. The second is the idea that a snake will chase you.

Grandma will swear that, as a child, a racer chased her from her house a half-mile to her grandmother's house. She was a small child and just riding her bike alone and going that far was adventure enough. She looked down and saw the snake. She took off, and the snake, according to her, followed. She bent over and peddled as fast as one of those little one-speed child bikes will go. One hazard always accompanied a bike ride. Getting your skirt or pant leg caught in the chain of the bike requiring a stop to untangle things. Sure enough, the chain ate the leg of her pants and brought her flight to a sudden stop. She was out of those pants in the blink of an eye and completed the last 100 yards of her race against death-by-snake in her skivvies.

Once at her grandmother's, she flew up the stairs to the porch and into the house. There she tearfully recited the story of her narrow escape to the appropriate hugs, sympathies, and freshly baked bread of a protective grandma.

Usually at that point I say, "Snakes won't chase you," at which she will retort, "It did chase me. I can still remember it like it was yesterday." Then a shiver will cross her face as she re-lives the event in her mind.

Because I can never win this discussion with her, I'll argue it here! The snake usually blamed for chasing people is the yellow-bellied racer. This is the only "racer" in North America, but because, like people, it comes in different colors, it has different names in different places.

Back east they call them blue racers or blacksnakes, and out west they are green racers. I've seen the blue version, and this summer I kept a green one in the dog pen for a month or so. Racers are slender snakes, rarely exceeding four feet in length (the record is about six feet). Most of them do have an aggressive temperament, and when handled they will thrash back and forth and bite vigorously. Despite that aggression, I think it is safe to say they virtually never eat people.

What racers feed on are small mammals, lizards, insects, and other snakes. Though their scientific name is *C. constrictor*, they don't constrict their prey at all. Racers swallow their meal whole, while that prey is still alive.

Racers are oviparous, which means they lay eggs. They will mate after emerging from hibernation in April and lay the eggs (about 15 of them) shortly thereafter. The eggs will incubate in the loose dirt and vegetation until late August and early September. Like most snakes, the adults do not care for the eggs or the young. Once the young snakes hatch, they don't look at all like the adults. They have the mottled, camouflage coloration similar to that of a bull snake or hognose snake. Racers grow quickly, and by the second or third year are fully-grown with the corresponding blue-green coloration.

Racers do live up to their name in one sense. They are fast…for a snake. How fast is that? Not very. A good high school sprinter can cover 100 meters in 10 seconds. That translates to about 21 miles per hour. Pretty fast. A small girl old enough to ride her bike a half mile can cover that distance in less than 30 seconds, which translates to seven miles per hour.

How long would it take the racer? If the racer could maintain top speed for the entire 100 yards, which is doubtful, it would take about a minute! Top speed for a "fast" snake is three miles per hour.

To add to the doubt the racer chased Grandma for a half mile is the fact that racers are the sprinters of the snake world, and sprinters who are initially fast usually lack much endurance. A snake, three–four feet long with a top speed of three miles per hour, will not be able to keep that speed up for more than 10 to 20 yards, and it is doubtful one would cover a half mile in less than a couple of hours.

To add further doubt to the idea that a racer would chase you is the question that if they eat their food whole, while alive, what would one do with you if it caught you? My mother-in-law is a small woman, but even the largest racer would have a mouth that would just fit over my thumb. Thus, there is nothing one of these small snakes could do with a person if in fact it did chase and catch her. So, given all that, I don't think snakes, at least snakes here in Nebraska, will chase you, but as I've said before, my mother-in-law would disagree.

Chapter 9:

SINGING THE SUN DOWN

I was sitting in the backyard with my wife, Cindy, and Lois, my mother-in-law, enjoying the late July evening. It was warm, but it was the kind of warm I dream about on those cold January nights with the snow flying and the wind howling. There was a light breeze, just enough to cool the skin and keep the mosquitoes at bay.

As the sun sank behind the trees to the west, a cicada started "singing," soon to be followed by another and yet another. The nightly Symphony of Summer had begun. Cicadas are one of a number of creatures that "sing" the sun down and the moon up each night.

The Symphony Season begins in late March with the chorus frogs, followed in April and May by a variety of birds and then in July and August by a myriad of insects. Along with the "bugs" are the toads trilling from the flooded road ditch and the bull frogs calling from the lake. However, on that warm summer night, it was the cicadas that held center stage.

"Katie did...Katie didn't," Lois said.

Cindy and I both looked at her. "What?"

"Katie did...Katie didn't," she repeated. "That's what katydids say: Katie did...Katie didn't."

"Except that isn't a katydid," I said.

"No," she said. "I know it's a locust, but it reminded me of the katydid saying."

The old biologist in me couldn't let that incorrect statement pass. "No, technically that isn't a locust. It's a cicada."

She looked at me, shook her head, and replied, "Aren't they the same thing?"

No…and yet, in a way, yes, they are. Katydids, locust, and cicadas have been misidentified by people throughout history. Katydids are a kind of grasshopper. They belong to the large group of grasshoppers called conehead or long-horned grasshoppers. The other group of grasshoppers are your typical grasshopper, which are called short horned grasshoppers. Technically speaking, it's the short horned grasshoppers that are locust, and then only under certain conditions is that term appropriate.

Then, to further confuse things, the family name for the katydids is Tettigoniidae which comes from the Greek 'tettly', which in English means 'cicada'. So it is understandable for someone to confuse a katydid with both a locust and with a cicada.

Using the incorrect name "locust" instead of the correct "cicada" came about from the early settlers in America and the Bible. Locust are common in the Middle East, and the Bible contains a number of references to plagues of locust, the most famous being the plague that Moses called down upon Egypt. Locust and other swarming insects, however, were not common in Europe, so the Europeans really didn't know what was meant by swarms of locust in the Bible.

When the European settlers came to America, they encountered the emergence of periodic cicadas. When the periodic cicadas emerge, they do so in surprising numbers. They cover trees, and they make a lot of noise. Unlike the locust of the Bible, the cicadas are not harmful. However, this was the closest thing to a "plague of locust" the European settlers had ever seen, and so they called them by that name.

Katydids and grasshoppers, belong to the order Orthoptera, or "straight winged" insects. Included with the katydids and grasshoppers are the crickets, praying mantis, walking sticks, and cockroaches.

Short horned grasshoppers here on the Great Plains periodically experience population explosions. It seems that when the populations get large enough and dense enough, that these grasshoppers will gather into swarms that move across the landscape eating everything in sight.

My father-in-law tells stories of the 30's when huge swarms of grasshoppers would descend upon the Platte Valley. He said grasshoppers would be so thick on fence posts there would literally be layers of them. Dean and his father would take the mules and a wagon around the fields. In a barrel in the back of the wagon they had a concoction of strychnine and molasses. Dean's dad would scoop out globs of the stuff onto the ground to attract and kill the insects. To this day, Dean cannot stand the smell of molasses.

On the front of the hay sweeps they had a ½ tank full of old oil and a screen. As the sweep moved through the hay field, the grasshoppers would jump up, hit the screen, and then fall into the oil. When so many grasshoppers were in the oil there was no more room, they would bun the oil and grasshoppers. Dean said that is another smell he will never forget. Grasshoppers were a big deal in the 30's!

When grasshoppers form the swarms that Dean describes, they are then rightfully called locust, and it was these kinds of swarms of grasshoppers that are referred to in the Bible.

Today, in an effort to prevent the formation of these huge swarms of 'hoppers, control (i.e. spraying with an insecticide) is practiced in most western states. This control is designed to keep the population of grasshoppers under the density threshold that apparently triggers the swarming activity. Here in Nebraska, there is a law called the Nebraska Rangeland Grasshopper Control Act, passed in 1938, that provides for some funding for grasshopper control so as to prevent the kind of population explosion that Dean remembers.

The katydids, or long horned grasshoppers, are more or less harmless, and for the most part they don't swarm. However, there is one variety, aptly known as the Mormon cricket, that will swarm, and it is this katydid that is the "locust" referred to in the story of the seagulls saving the early Mormons in Utah.

According to the story, in 1848 the crops of the Mormon settlers in the Salt Lake Valley in Utah were being decimated by a plague of locust. Just as all the crops were about to be lost, large numbers of gulls flew in and started to eat the locust. The Mormons saw the arrival of the gulls as God's answer to their prayers, and the saved crops made it possible for the Mormons to survive the ensuing winter. In Salt Lake there is a monument to this episode in Mormon history and the role of the gulls in saving the colony.

Crickets, grasshoppers, and katydids all make sounds through a process called stridulation. This is a process of rubbing one wing or leg against the other. The sounds, like the songs of birds, are distinguishable, and each makes a unique sound. Crickets also change the rate of stridulation based upon the temperature, so you can actually estimate temperature by how rapidity the cricket chirps.

Cicadas are quite different from the grasshoppers and katydids. They belong to the insect group Homoptera, or the "same winged" insects. There are two basic kinds of cicadas. The most famous are the 17-year and 13-year periodical cicadas. These are forest insects that as nymphs live underground, feeding on the fluids from tree roots. After their allotted 17 or 13 years they emerge as a group, molt into adults, sing, mate, and lay eggs, starting the process all over again. Periodical cicadas typically emerge in May and June, and they are striking in appearance. They are black with red eyes and orange wings. When they emerge, they do so in large numbers, thus leading the early settlers to believe these were the locust plagues of the Bible.

In the United States, there are seven different species of periodical cicadas and all are found in the east and southeast. The species are then further broken into "broods." Each brood emerges during specific years, and they are identified using Roman Numerals. Brood Number I, for example, is found in Virginia and West Virginia, and they emerged during 2012. This summer along the east coast it is Brood Number II. Nebraska's only brood of periodical cicadas, Brood Number IV, is found in the far south-eastern portion of the state. They last emerged in 2015 and are expected to emerge again in 2032.

The other kind of cicada, the one common throughout Nebraska, is the annual cicada, and that is what we were listening to in the backyard. The annual cicadas live as nymphs underground, feeding on the sap from tree roots for two, three, or even five years. They then crawl up the side of the tree, molt into their adult form, and then begin to sing, mate, lay eggs, and die.

Because the life cycles of the annual cicadas all overlap, we have some emerging each and every year, hence the name. Another name for the annual cicadas, and probably a more descriptive name, is the Dog-Day Cicada, as they emerge during the "dog-days" of late summer.

The Dog-Day Cicadas tend to be larger than the periodical cicadas and are green and black in appearance. The male will try and attract the female with his "song." Unlike the katydid, which rubs its wings together to make noise, the male cicada has a drum-like structure called the timbale on the side of its abdomen. The timbale is a thin membrane stretched over solid, thickened strands of the exoskeleton. When the cicada contracts the membrane, the thickened strands bend and click. When the timbale is relaxed, the strands click again as they return to their normal shape. The rabid contraction and relaxation gives us the familiar clicking song of late summer.

There is a folk tale that the first frost of the year will be six weeks after the cicadas start to sing. This is more-or-less true. In Nebraska, the cicadas emerge and begin singing in early August with the average first frost date ranging from around the 10th of September in the west and north to early October in the southeast—thus six to eight weeks later. This year I heard my first cicada on July 5th. Six weeks from that is mid-August. Let's hope the folk tale is wrong!

Any number of things eat cicadas, and in fact, they were common in the diet of Native Americans. However the worst nightmare for a cicada is a wasp called the cicada killer.

Cicada killers are a form of parasitic wasp. Parasitic wasps feed on spiders, caterpillars, and other insects, and their life cycles are all pretty much the same. The cicada killer is a wasp that specializes in eating cicadas. This wasp is huge, and in fact, it is Nebraska's largest wasp. However, it is not aggressive and rarely stings unless bothered.

The wasp finds a cicada in the trees and stings it. The sting carries a paralyzing agent. The now helpless and paralyzed cicada is carried by the wasp to a burrow the wasp has dug. She pulls and pushes the live, paralyzed cicada down into a side chamber of the burrow and then lays an egg on its body. In some forms of parasitic wasps, the egg is laid inside the body.

The female cicada killer then leaves and hunts down another cicada, drags it back to the burrow, and repeats the process. The burrow contains a number of cicadas when she is done.

When the eggs hatch, the larvae emerge and start to eat the paralyzed cicada alive. Usually the larva feeds in such a way as to actually preserve the life of the cicada as long as possible so that the "meat" does not rot.

Once the larva has devoured the entire cicada, it forms a pupa and remains in the burrow through the winter. It emerges again the next summer when the next round of cicadas, crickets, and katydids will once again emerge and sing to sleep the late summer sun.

Chapter 10:

SNAILS

I read a great deal, and in reading I discover any number of things. Yet, the things I discover out along the river, walking through the hills, or even emptying the garbage seem to have a bigger impact on my thinking and in stimulating my curiosity than do any of the wonders that I find between the pages of Janovy, Thoreau, Leopold, or Abby.

If I'm able to discover something on my own, something that one of these writers may have also discovered and discussed in their musings, it makes an even greater impact on me. That was exactly what happened when I was out emptying the garbage a few years ago.

My neighbor was having a problem with groundwater. The water was seeping into his basement. In an effort to prevent his family room from becoming an indoor swimming pool, he installed a gravel drain field around the house with a pump to eliminate the water.

When he contacted the City about pumping this water directly into the sewage system, he was told it would cost an $800 hook-up fee and that he would then have a second monthly water and sewage bill. Instead, he connected a few links of plastic pipe together to take the water across his backyard, under the alley and to the pasture that lies to the south of our block. The owner of the pasture gave his okay, so there wasn't a problem.

The pump runs almost continuously. Cold, gravel-filtered water pours out of the opening in the pipe and down a small constructed ditch in the pasture to the street where it then flows down hill to the corner and enters a storm drain—a way around the rules of the City.

I was taking out the trash one evening in May when I noticed something in the ditch. Snails. Snails were in the cold groundwater coming from my neighbor's drain field. I looked around. It was at least a half-mile to the nearest standing water. How had the snails made their way from that water across the arid, overgrazed calving pasture to this ditch, and more importantly, why had they made their way to this spot?

As those questions rattled around in my head, I remembered someone else, 20 years ago, asking the same question. John Janovy Jr. wrote about it in his book, *Keith County Journal*. He looked at snails in windmill tanks in the middle of the Sandhills and wondered how they had made their way across the prairie to the tank. His book is one that should be required reading for all would-be biologists and any lover of nature. Equally important for all would-be biologists and/or lovers of nature is to get into the water, waist deep, and look eye-to-eye with a snail (yes, they have eyes) and ponder the same question.

Snails are one of nature's most prolific creatures. Most species are hermaphroditic, which means they are both boys and girls. Some are boys for a time, but then they turn into girls. Others reverse the trend. Most are both throughout their lives. Some can self-fertilize. Most, however, though hermaphrodites, must mate with another. Talk about your confusing parental lineage. As one writer put it, imagine that your sister's mom is your dad and her dad is your mom.

Being hermaphroditic allows the snails to take advantage of two reproductive strategies. Sexual reproduction provides a species with genetic diversity that allows for a greater chance for success in a wide variety of environments. However, sexual reproduction requires the finding of a mate. This means finding an individual not only of the same species but also one of the opposite sex. This is a significant problem for an animal as small as a snail which doesn't cover much area over the course of its life.

Asexual reproduction eliminates that problem because it does not require a mate. However, asexual reproduction also does not provide the genetic variation so valuable in the colonization of new environments.

Being hermaphroditic, snails have simplified the reproduction process and made it twice as profitable. They only have to find a member of the same species—any member, any time, any place, and they can mate. Following that, not just one, but both snails will produce thousands of eggs, much like asexually reproducing creatures, yet each and every egg will have a new and unique mix of genetic information, making each and every snail slightly different. If they meet another snail, they mate again, and again both snails produce eggs.

This produces a lot, a whole lot, of offspring, so many offspring that not all can possibly survive in the ponds or streams of their parents. Thus, snails make excellent pioneers. Given their potential for overpopulation, the snails must have a way of striking out to inhabit new territory. There, if their unique genetic mix matches the environment, some will survive. Most, however, die out. This has two advantages. First, it is a "check" on the population size of the species, and second, it allows for the colonization of new environments.

Given a successful mechanism of travel, the snails, over time, will inhabit just about any suitable aquatic environment. Thus, the "why" of finding their way to the ditch is answered in their reproductive biology. But the "how" is not answered. Just how does an animal that "doesn't cover much area over the course of its life" act as a pioneer to new environs?

Just as their reproductive biology gives me the "why," other aspects of their natural history answer the "how." In fact, it answers both why and how they are found in almost all water bodies in Nebraska except those that are severely polluted or extremely salty. It answers why they are in the rivers, sloughs, sandpits, marshes, rainwater basin lakes, windmill tanks in the middle of the sandhills, and in a small man-made canal behind my house.

The snails in the ditch belong to the genus (large group) of snails called *Physia*. I italicized the word because it is the "official Latin name" of the group. Biologists worldwide will know I'm talking about common pond snails. I don't know what species they are. I really don't want to know. In some snails, you have to take a microscopic look at their reproductive organs to identify species. I'm not sure who figured that out, but I'll take his/her word for it. I'll just be satisfied that I can identify the genus.

That's actually quite easy to do with *Physia* because they are *Sinistral* while the other common aquatic snails here in central Nebraska are either flattened into a "ram's horn" shape, or are *Dextral*. Sinistral and dextral refer to which side the opening in the shell is on. If you hold a snail so that the point of the shell is up and the body opening is facing you, sinistral means the opening is to the left and dextral means it opens to the right.

Of the five species of aquatic snails found in the Platte valley by Keith Perkins in his survey of the river in 1992 and 1993, three (*Gyraulus*, *Helisoma*, and *Planorbula*) have the coiled ram's horn appearance while *Physia* is sinistral and a snail called *Stagnicola* (the "official Latin name" for the stagnant pond snail) is dextral.

Physia are air breathers. They take air into a lung-like cavity where it is then exchanged with the body tissues. They can also take oxygen directly from the water through their skin; however, most of their active respiration occurs while they are at the surface

This means they can withstand temporary drying of their environment, or live completely submerged. They eat live or decaying plant material, and *Physia* has been known to feed on carrion. Thus, *Physia* can live in just about any aquatic environment, something critical for a pioneer. However the most important point in answering my question about how they move from one water body to the other lies in their eggs. A covering of slime protects *Physia* eggs. Slime protects the young snail as it goes through its development before hatching into a miniature adult

The slimy covering also makes the eggs sticky. Because the adult snails are laying eggs just about everywhere, in the vegetation of a pond, lake, windmill tank, or ditch, when a bird steps into the ditch, it steps into snail eggs. Where the bird goes, the eggs go. Like my boy tracking mud across his mother's kitchen floor, shorebirds and waterfowl "track" snail eggs across any and all wetted surfaces.

That's not bad mobility for something moving at (I can't help it) a snail's pace, a mobility that makes them common animals in a semiarid state like Nebraska and that has a biologist somewhere, miles from any other water source, knee deep in organic-rich pond water, eye-to-eye with them asking, "How did these snails get here?"

Chapter 11:
POISON IVY

It's funny, in a way, what makes a person start thinking about something or other. Usually, for me, it involves a personal experience, however that isn't always enough. I also have to have some peripheral thing that focuses my mind on a concept, which happens to relate to the personal experience. Take poison ivy, for example.

I'm not a botanist, and I don't generally think much about plants, including poison ivy. My botany professor was great, and he did try to instill in me a love for plants. But, alas, those lessons were lost. My college roommate, Dahlas—now he was a plant guy. Where I had snakes, rats, and spiders in jars on the dresser, he had plants growing in the window. He loved the challenge of knowing and identifying all the different kinds of grasses and non-descript broadleaf plants that make up the Nebraska prairie. He didn't care that plants didn't wiggle, bite, or go to the bathroom on you. He just loved the darn things. He also loved it when someone else couldn't identify a plant, especially when that plant was poison ivy. I still recall the fun he had identifying poison ivy for an outfitter on the Niobrara River. The outfitter had the gear of twenty people piled alongside the river south of Ninzel, Nebraska, gear that belonged to a group from the Sierra Club of Nebraska. He was waiting for his charges, lying in the lush green foliage with his head propped up on a sleeping bag; reading.

Dahlas walked over and in an innocent voice asked if the guy knew what poison ivy looked like. When the outfitter answered that, yes, he did, Dahlas then asked him why he was lying in it and why he had all that gear piled in it.

We had a good laugh for the first mile or two down the river recalling the hurry and scurry of the outfitter to move all that gear. Of course we never did hear if the Sierra Club folks took home an unwanted memory of their float down the Niobrara.

What goes around comes around, and for Dahlas and me that was true. He and I were annually tasked with the responsibility of fighting thistle and fixing fence on his family's ranch in Custer County (me having married his sister). We came upon a 50-foot stretch of fence that needed replacement. The wire was down, and some of the posts were broken. The only problem was that the fence ran right through a huge patch of ivy. I remember telling Dahlas that I had never been bothered by poison ivy before. He related that he hadn't either, so we dove in.

Two days later, he was back home in Lincoln, I was in Gothenburg. We were both miserable. Never again would either of us state that we were not affected by poison ivy. As vivid as these two experiences are in my mind, neither prompted me to learn anything about poison ivy. I simply accepted the lack of observation by the outfitter and Dahlas' and my stupidity and moved on in life, until the right set of circumstances occurred.

It started with me being back on the Niobrara River. I was with Craig and Kristen, their two daughters, and two other couples and their kids (My wife not being a canoeist and the boys being a bit too young at the time, they stayed home). Kristen and I went exploring in the area looking for snails. We didn't find any snails, but we did find liverwort, the only time I've ever seen it outside of the biology lab, and poison ivy. Well, we didn't find the ivy, Kristen did.

As it happens I had just completed a refresher course in the theories of evolution and had been doing some extensive reading about the concept of change through time by species. When I talked with Craig later that summer he related to me Kristen's two weeks of misery upon returning home from the float. It was then that I started thinking about poison ivy.

Based on what I had been reading about evolution and natural selection, I made the mistake of immediately jumping to the conclusion that poison ivy secreted a material on its surface to inhibit grazing and other disturbance and that it was this material that caused the problem. But in order to prove to myself that I was correct, I had to become intellectually familiar with the plant. As I indicated earlier, I had already become physically familiar with it.

I already knew that poison ivy was one of a number of plants that cause an allergic reaction in people. A member of the sumac family, it's related to poison oak and poison sumac. Even I have to admit it is very attractive. It consists of woody, underground stems and above ground vines. The leaves grow in dark, lush green clusters (usually three, sometimes five), and it can be found as a ground cover growing over large areas. It can also be a vine growing up and over fences and on trees. During the 19th century, it was cultivated here in the U.S. and in England as a garden plant. Of course, at that time they hadn't pieced together the fact that it was the ivy that was responsible for the horrible rash that the gardeners endured.

In the spring, the plants produce flowers that develop into clusters of white, waxy berries. These berries and the woody stems that support the leaves can also cause the allergic response in people. In the fall, the leaves of the plant turn a rusty to bright red and, along with the white berries, they are very colorful.

Poison ivy contains a resin that is allergenic to humans but apparently causes little or no problem with other creatures. These same resins are found in cashew nut plants, Ginkgo's, mangos, and the plant that produces India Ink.

Contrary to what I thought, this resin is internal. It's not found on the surface of the plant. Thus you don't come in contact with the oil simply by touching the plant. You have to injure the fragile stems or bruise the leaves by walking through the plants. The resin then leaks out, and that's when you come in contact with it.

Thus my first misconception of the function of the oil in the life of the plant proved to be false. I thought it was a protective mechanism to inhibit grazing by animals. However, since most animals are not affected by it and its effects are delayed by a day or two, even if that were its purpose, it wouldn't be very effective.

It seems to inhibit fungus and may be a protective fluid to prevent infection within the plant when the outer skin is broken. A second function is that it dries, hardens, and seals a wound in the skin of the plant much like the scab that forms over small cuts and abrasions on our own skins. The oil, it turns out, is simply a chemical that, like ragweed pollen, penicillin, and cat saliva, is allergenic to people.

When you first get the resin on your skin, all is not lost. It doesn't have any effect on the surface and has to first diffuse through this tough outer layer of the epidermis and get to a group of cells that are found at the bottom of the outer layer of skin. This takes time. Generally, you have 10–15 minutes in which you can wash it off. Cool water actually works best because warm water causes an opening in skin pores that can allow the resin to penetrate to the lower layers.

Strangely enough, these cells actually metabolize the resin and produce a waste product from it. This waste product is the substance that, for some reason or other, our bodies will not tolerate and our immune systems attack.

Our body has a variety of defense strategies to attack and kill unwanted materials and creatures within our bodies. One is to release chemicals that destroy the material. Unfortunately, these chemicals also destroy the surrounding tissue. That tissue destruction is the rash we experience.

Scratching the rash will not spread the condition—unless there is still resin on the surface of the skin. You can also compound the problem if the resin is on your clothes, the dog, or car seat. The semi-dried resin can remain viable on your skin or clothes for 12–15 days under the right conditions.

How severe your reaction to poison ivy is depends upon your sensitivity to the resin and the quantity of resin with which you come into contact. There are lotions you can put on to prevent the resin from contacting the skin, and a vaccine is being developed which may free us from the need to worry about coming in contact with the plant. However, today, if you go snail hunting, fence fixing, or river floating and inadvertently come in contact with poison ivy or one of its cousins, there are treatments, but for the most part, you basically just have to put up with it for the next two weeks.

I had envisioned a complex evolutionary response by poison ivy plants as a mechanism for protection. I was wrong. Instead, it seems the misery from poison ivy is caused by some waste product produced by our own bodies. I'm disappointed, but if nothing else, Dahlas' and my botany teacher will be proud of me. I actually studied about a plant. Next thing you know I'll have one of the dadgum things growing on the windowsill here in the office!

Chapter 12:
DRAGONFLIES

Last weekend, the weather was so nice that I took a quiet walk down by the river. I really wasn't looking for anything, so when I heard the small "plop" of the frog, I decided to stop and wait by the side of this small pond. The river began dropping about a month ago, leaving this low-lying pond behind. While the water was still fairly clear, there were floating mats of green algae beginning to form along with the trapped fish and a variety of other animals, including, apparently, a frog.

I decided to stop for no other reason than to identify the kind of frog that had jumped into the pond. I sat down. By being still, I knew I could fool the small amphibian. It would come back to the surface, and then I could determine what kind it was.

Sitting still has other rewards. I watched the small backswimmers (aquatic insects) moving across and through the clear water and the tiger beetles foraging along the bank. I listened to the warble of the wren and the call of the flitting chickadees as they moved through the trees. However, what was most enjoyable was watching the dragonfly.

If there is water around, there will probably be dragonflies. In fact, dragonflies are so common that just about anyone and everyone can identify them. However, there are some 413 species of dragonflies in the United States with more than 50 species here in Nebraska. While most people can identify a dragonfly, knowing what species of dragonfly it is takes a bit more expertise!

Dragonflies belong to the Order Odonata. There are two suborders. The dragonflies, or Anisoptera (in English that means unequal wings), are mostly large and robust and can be recognized when they land because they hold their wings horizontally, straight out from their body. The members of the second suborder, the damselflies (If you have a dragon, you must have a damsel!) or Zygoptera (symmetrical wings), are more delicate. They are slower fliers, and when they land, they hold their wings folded vertically like that of a butterfly.

As nymphs, you can also tell the difference between the dragonflies and damselflies. The dragonfly nymph, like the adult, is large and robust, and it has three very small tube-like projections on the tip of its abdomen. These surround the opening to the rectum. Inside the rectum, there are a number of small tubes in the walls, which are called tracheal gills. The dragonfly draws water into the rectum where it moves over and through the tracheal gills, and "breathing" occurs.

Once the exchange of oxygen for carbon dioxide occurs, the water is expelled from the rectum. This expulsion can be quite explosive, causing the nymph to "jet" through the water.

The damselfly nymphs are not rectum breathers. Instead they have three long, feather-like projections from their abdomen. These are gills that move back and forth though the water. Not only does this movement keep fresh water moving over the surface of the gill, effecting gas exchange, but it also causes the nymph to move in a graceful, undulating way.

Dragonflies and damselflies are some of the most important insect predators that can be found in and around any wetland area. They are voracious feeders, making a basket with their legs in which they catch hundreds of gnats, mosquitoes, and other small flying insects each day of their adult lives.

The dragonfly I watched was not hunting, however. She was flying here and there over the surface of the pond, all the while dipping the tip of her abdomen down to just touch the surface of the water. She was laying eggs. As I watched, she zigzagged across the surface, moving from one end of the pond to the other. In one minute's time, she touched the surface of the water 36 times.

The eggs will hatch in about 10 days. In some species, the eggs are deposited later in the year and overwinter on the bottom of the pond before hatching. Once hatched, the young dragonfly, called the nymph, doesn't look anything like an adult. Nymphs feed on other aquatic insects (including dragonfly nymphs), snails, small crustaceans and even small fish on the bottom of the pool. Like the adult form, the dragonfly nymph is an important predator in the aquatic community.

Upon completion of its development, the larvae will crawl up on a stick or plant growing out of the water, molt, and fly off as an adult dragonfly. Dragonfly larvae may live up to four years in the rotting vegetation at the bottom of the pond, feeding on the other aquatic insects that are found there. During that time, they may go through as many as 15 different stages before crawling out of the water to molt into the adult stage. Like most insects, the adult stage in the life of a dragonfly doesn't last that long. The adult male may take two weeks to become sexually mature. Once mature, they become very aggressive. They stake out a territory and defend it from any and all other males. If a female enters the territory, the male will mate with her. This period of aggression lasts for about 10 days to two weeks, at the end of which the adults, mating and egg-laying completed, die. Unlike many insects that as adults do not eat, the dragonflies consume thousands of small flying insects during this month of adulthood.

Mating in dragonflies is complicated and interesting. The sperm of the male is transferred twice. Once produced, the male transfers the sperm packet from the pore at the end of the abdomen to the secondary sex organs, which are located on the other end of the abdomen, just under the base of the thorax. This frees the distal (far) end of the abdomen, which contains special appendages for the grasping of the female. The male then grasps the female by the head using these specially adapted structures. The female then curves her abdomen up to the secondary sex organs of the male where the sperm is then transferred again, this time to the female. This may take a few minutes, or the two may stay fixed "in tandem" for an extended period of time. Once the eggs are fertilized, the female then begins to lay them. In some species, the male keeps his hold on the female until she has completed the egg laying process. This prevents other males from mating with the female and in the process scooping the sperm from the first male out and replacing it with his own.

The dragonfly I was watching was an eastern pondhawk, a midsized dragonfly that is common here in the valley. As I watched the dragonfly scattering her eggs, reviewing what I knew about these wonderful insects, I suddenly realized I had forgotten about the frog. Moving only my eyes, I searched the algae mat growing on the surface of the pond, and there it was. Without my noticing it, the frog had come back to the surface, and there it laid, eyes and nostrils above the surface and the rest of its body splayed out below. It was a small bullfrog.

I stood, sending the frog back to the bottom of the pond to snuggle beneath the security of the rotting leaves and other detritus. The dragonfly flew off to another pond. I brushed the sand from my legs and picked a sandbur from my jeans. I had suspected the frog would be a bullfrog, and I was correct. I could have kept walking. Verifying the frog was a bullfrog accomplished nothing, except it was by waiting out the frog that I got to watch the tiger beetles, listen to the wren, and contemplate the life history of dragonflies.

Chapter 13:
POOR MAN'S LOBSTER

The water didn't feel as cold today. Last week there was snow flying and ice forming on the surface where the water contacted the concrete of the tailrace, but today spring was in full force—a typical Nebraska Spring. The air temperature was almost 70 degrees, where as last week it had been in the teens with 35-mph winds from the northwest. I don't think the water was really any warmer, but because it was so much nicer outside, it felt warmer.

We made our measurements of the width and of the diagonal of the tailrace opening, and Kent and I were now resting on the floor of the tailrace waiting for the signal from above that our job was complete and that we could go up.

The "tailrace" is the concrete chute leading from the powerhouse downstream to the canal. The water enters the powerhouse at the "fore bay" and passes down the "penstock" through the turbines where it generates the electricity, and then it leaves the plant through the tailrace.

The plant is the Johnson #2 Powerhouse, and we were making preliminary measurements in preparation for the renovation that the Central Nebraska Public Power and Irrigation District had planned for the powerhouse. Large, heavy gates would be constructed and placed in the grooves in the sides of the tailrace so that the water can be pumped completely out of the plant when the renovation occurred. It was important to know if the opening was "square," so they asked Kent and me to put on our SCUBA equipment, heavy neoprene wetsuits, and take a tape into the water and make the measurements.

We had already measured at Central's other Johnson Lake powerhouse and the one south of Brady at Jeffrey Lake. The J-2 Plant, as it's referred to, was the last. As I stated, it wasn't as cold as it had been when we did our dives at the other plants, so I didn't mind having to wait 25 feet under water. Another reason I didn't mind the wait was the crayfish—not one crayfish, not a few crayfish, not even quite a few crayfish. The floor of the tailrace, which is water-polished concrete, was literally crawling with hundreds if not thousands of crayfish.

We couldn't put our hands or knees down without touching them, so I floated just off the bottom and watched. Taking the power plant offline for an extended period of time coupled with the improvement in the weather resulted in fairly calm, clear water below the plant. The warming, clear water must have triggered the urge to reproduce in the crayfish as mating pairs were more common than lone individuals.

Most of the individuals were males. You can tell the sex of a crayfish in the same way that you do dogs and cats. You look under the back legs. The tail of the crayfish is broken into segments. Each segment has two appendages called "swimmerets". When the female lays her eggs, the eggs stick to these swimmerets, and she carries them with her. This gives the eggs a measure of protection against egg-eating fish and other creatures. Once the eggs hatch, the young crayfish hang on to the swimmerets until they have grown large enough to set out on their own.

The males also have swimmerets and it's the difference in the male swimmerets and those of the female that allows you to tell boy from girl. On the male, the swimmerets on the first and second segments of the tail (the ones closest to the body) are quite long and fold forward up the groove in the belly of the crayfish. On the female, the swimmerets on the first two segments are not elongated, and you can easily see the genital pore.

Crayfish are like lobsters. In fact, crayfish are lobsters. They are freshwater lobsters. Lobsters and crayfish, along with shrimp and about 26,000 other kinds of animals are crustaceans. Crustaceans are mostly aquatic animals, and they can be distinguished from the other arthropods (insects, spiders, and such) by the fact they have a head, thorax, and segmented tail or abdomen. Attached to the head are two pairs of antennae along with a number of appendages for the gathering and chewing of food. On the thorax, there are five pairs of legs. In crayfish, the first pair are modified into large claws which are used for protection and for battles over territory with other crayfish.

The other four pairs are walking legs. The first two walking legs have small claws, and in addition to walking, the crayfish use these for feeling around in the rocks and gravel on the bottom of the pond for food.

At the other end of each walking leg is a gill. In most crustaceans, the gills are feather-like structures that are found outside the body, swaying in the water. In crayfish, these feather-like appendages are hooked to the top of the leg so that each time the leg moves, the gill moves. This movement back and forth through the water insures a fresh supply of oxygenated water over the surface of the gill. Covering the gill and protecting it from harm is the carapace, or shell of the crayfish.

Though the carapace gives the gills and the rest of the animal protection, it also presents a problem. As the animal grows, the shell, which is dead material, must be shed and a new shell secreted. Thus, the crayfish must molt. While molting, the animal's soft body is not protected, and until the new shell hardens, it is vulnerable to predation and a variety of parasites. Another problem with molting deals with the crayfish's mechanism for maintaining balance.

On the head of the crayfish, along with the eyes, there are two sets of antennae. The smaller set, called the antennules, function as sensory organs and are important in maintaining balance. There are small openings at the base of these appendages. Inside the openings, there are structures called statocysts. These consist of a small chamber lined with hair-like projections similar to what are found in the inner ear of humans. The hair-like projections are the ends of nerves projecting through the tissue wall. The crayfish place a small rock in this chamber, and the position of the rock against the hair-like nerve endings of the statocysts tell the crayfish up from down.

When the crayfish molts, the inner lining of this opening is sloughed off, and the small rock is lost. The crayfish must then insert a new rock into the opening in order to maintain its balance. Scientists, in studying balance and the inner ears of humans, used crayfish for research. They found that if you put iron filings in the bottom of the aquarium where the crayfish are housed, upon molting the crayfish put these small pieces of iron in the opening at the base of the antennules. The piece of iron functions in the same way as a rock, that is, until a strong magnet is brought close to the crayfish. The iron, when pulled toward the magnet, results in pressure on a different area of nerve endings, which then "tell" the crayfish that the direction toward the magnet is "down." The crayfish will then adjust itself accordingly, even if that means lying on the bottom, upside down.

Crayfish are capable of learning, and the pressure of the rock or piece of iron inside the statocyst is not the only input to their small brain telling them up from down. In time, the crayfish will right itself and become acclimated to the change in "down" caused by the magnet. Once they noted the crayfish had acclimated itself to the new "down," the researchers then took the magnet away. Gravity once again was the strongest force acting on the iron, and the small piece settled to the real down. The crayfish, having adjusted to the new "down," then adjusts itself…upside down again. You can almost imagine the fun these biologists had, constantly changing the poor crayfish's concept of "down." Talk about motion sickness! I wonder if crayfish can throw up?

There are over 200 different kinds of crayfish in the U.S., but we only have four or five different kinds here in Nebraska. The low diversity of crayfish is a reflection of the natural climate of the state. We are a prairie state without extensive shallow water swamps and wetlands. However, in the lakes, rivers, and wetlands that do exist, there are usually a lot of individual crayfish.

Like anything else, different kinds of crayfish are different in size. The ones here in Nebraska are average-sized. However, they are big enough to eat, and to some that's what is important about a crayfish. There are a variety of ways to fix poor man's lobster. The most common way is soak the live crayfish in clean water for a day or so. You then dump them into boiling salt water while still alive. After boiling, you pour them out, twist or cut off the tails, shell them, pull out the vein, dip them in butter or a sauce, and eat. You can also use them in a number of Cajun casseroles, sauces, and soups. When in Louisiana a couple of years ago at a conference, we literally ate crayfish etouffee every day.

Crayfish have other values, both positive and negative. To the fisherman, they are viewed as bass bait, while to a biologist they are an important aquatic scavenger. High School biology students use them as dissection specimens, and siphon tube irrigators cuss them when they clog up a tube.

Crayfish can also cause problems with dikes and levees. They dig long burrows in the mud just under the water surface. These burrows can weaken the dike, which in turn may lead to the dike or levee failing.

The canal below the powerhouse is a perfect place for crayfish. It has a mud bottom, and there is an abundance of rock, concrete, and old appliances and other junk littering the bottom of the ditch. The crayfish can live in and among the junk, feeding on the abundant supply of rotting vegetation, insect larvae, dead fish, and all the other things a scavenger finds tasty.

However, I wasn't thinking of those things as I lay there in the 43-degree water waiting for the signal from above telling Kent and me that it was time to surface. I was thinking how amazing it was that so many had gathered here in such a relatively short time and how we hadn't seen any at the other two plants. I was also thinking about how surprised those amorous little lobsters were going to be when we brought the plant back on line. They were definitely going to be in for one wild ride.

Chapter 14:

EAGLES IN THE ROOST

There are a couple of ways to conduct bald eagle roost surveys. One is to walk into the area during the dying light of the afternoon sun, find a comfortable spot, and settle in. From there, you can observe the birds coming to the roost. You remain until after dark and then find your way out. This is a lot of fun, especially if you have an interest in eagle behavior. When the birds come to the roost there is a lot of interaction. They fight over the best roost sites, do a lot of calling, and generally put on a show.

A different method is to wait until it is good and dark and then night-hike into the roost. This second method doesn't require as much time because all the birds will be at the roost when you get there, so you don't have to stick around very long. Walking in after dark, you can get much closer to the trees the eagles are using. But, then again, you have to get closer because it's so dark you won't be able to count them otherwise.

That is what my boys and I had done. We were leaning on a downed cottonwood tree that had recently been felled by a beaver, possibly the same beaver that had repeatedly slapped the water's surface as we made our way along the river to this spot.

Our walk had taken us from the pickup through about 500 yards of dogwood, plum, small willows, young cottonwoods, old cottonwoods, cedars, dead limbs, and other downfall.

Walking in the dark, because flashlights might disturb the birds, we had picked our way through this maze of obstacles for the last 10 minutes. Trying to move silently, trying to keep from tripping, and trying not to walk face-first into a sharp branch had proven to be a bit of a challenge.

As we stood there, relaxing and catching our breaths, I counted the birds in the roost tree. The 10 X 80 binoculars helped me see the eagles against the lighter, star-filled sky.

As I was counting, Reece, my oldest son, tapped my arm and whispered, "Dad, there's more over there."

Sure enough, in a tree across the small side channel, eight more eagles were visible. Using the binoculars, I scanned the opposite shore and found yet a third tree packed with birds…15, 16, 17, 18 more eagles. There were seven in the tree on our side of the channel and eight in one tree across the channel and 18 in the other. Thirty-three eagles, the highest count I've ever had at this roost. Last year's count was eleven during this same time period.

Thirty-three eagles in one spot is a lot when you consider that a state-wide survey 45 years ago found only 60 for all of Nebraska. Since then, the bald eagle population has made a remarkable recovery. It wasn't the recovery of their population that prompted me to write about eagles, however. It was the crowding together of thirty-three birds in an area the size of a typical backyard that initiated these thoughts, a crowding that seems odd considering eagles are so territorial during the summer. Why the change? Why, during the breeding season, will eagles attack any other eagle within a mile of the nest, yet during the winter they'll crowd together, wingtip to wingtip, in the same group of trees? The answer is food!

During the summer, the eagles not only feed themselves, they also feed their young, and that takes a lot of food. By defending their territory, they insure that the food available within that territory is not utilized by some other nesting pair. However, even with a large territory, food can be scarce, and problems can arise.

Eagles, like many birds of prey, lay one egg and then delay the laying of the next egg for a few days. They do, however, start incubating as soon as the first egg is in the nest. If a third egg is produced, it is laid in the nest a few days after the second egg. When the eggs hatch, the first one will hatch a few days before the second, which will hatch a few days before the third.

The first chick grows rapidly and is much larger than its younger siblings. If the older chick is a female and the younger a male, the size difference is even more pronounced as female eagles are usually larger than the males.

When food is brought to the nest by the parents, the largest chick is usually fed first. Thus if there isn't enough food for two or three chicks, the first to hatch, the biggest chick, is insured food, continues to grow, and has the best chance of survival. The smaller bird doesn't get enough food, doesn't grow as rapidly, and may starve.

Under the best of conditions, the young birds are naturally aggressive towards each other. If the birds are not well fed and one of the chicks is weaker and smaller, the bigger chick may become so aggressive that it drives the weaker bird from the nest and occasionally out-and-out kills it. If food is plentiful, both chicks are well fed, making the larger bird less aggressive, and the smaller bird can defend itself.

With a larger territory, there is a greater potential to find food. More food means more chicks will survive, and the more chicks the eagles can successfully raise, the better for the population as a whole. Thus, during the summer being territorial is a good thing.

During the winter, finding food really becomes a problem. Ponds, lakes, and rivers ice over, and what food is available may be concentrated in isolated areas that are hard to locate. A different strategy is needed. Eagles feed mainly on fish. If fish are not available, the eagles will prey on sick or wounded waterfowl or carrion. If necessary, they will hunt rabbits and other small mammals. Active hunting, however, is very energy expensive and over the long run does not benefit the eagles. Thus finding an area of open water, a bunch of geese, or a dead deer is crucial for the birds. In order to find the open water, geese, or carrion, the eagles resort to some of the same tactics as do vultures.

The key to the behavior of vultures and wintering eagles is communication. The birds communicate with others in many ways. One is by soaring. Hawks, eagles, and vultures have excellent eyesight, far better than you or I. When they soar, they can see, and be seen by other birds miles away.

If one eagle spots a potential food source, it will alter its flight profile. The other eagles note this alteration, and they alter their flight paths and profiles in order to bring them closer to the first bird. Still other eagles note the changes made by these birds and alter their flights respectively. In a short period of time, birds are drawn to the food source from as far away as thirty-to-forty miles. This can be seen in Nebraska as bald eagles routinely move from Sutherland Reservoir 30 miles west to Lake Ogallala below Kingsley Dam and back, or westward another 20 miles to the Clear Creek Refuge on the west end of Lake McConaughy.

This may seem counter-productive to the eagle that first sees the food source. More birds should equal less for the finder to eat. However, in winter, food sources don't last long. Eagles are only one of a number of predators and/or scavengers that will take advantage of the food source. For example, I once picked up a road-kill deer and placed it in a meadow near an eagle roost. My purpose was to photograph eagles. It took nine days for virtually every scrap of that deer to disappear. In those nine days, I only saw eagles there once. Most of the deer disappeared during the nighttime. Thus it's an advantage to the eagles as a group to have as many utilize that food source as possible before the coyotes and other nighttime scavengers take their share.

Some biologists believe another way the birds may communicate is at the communal roosts. An eagle that is well fed is more docile and less aggressive than one that is hungry. They fly to the roost and conduct preening and other actions consistent with well-being. The hungry eagles note this behavior, and it's believed they will then follow the well-fed bird the next day. The eagles tend to return to the same area year after year and have learned where food can usually be found. Through the communal roost, they are able to teach the younger birds where these areas are located.

Because of this vulture-like behavior, Benjamin Franklin didn't approve of the bald eagle as our National Emblem. He also didn't like the fact that during the winter bald eagles really don't do much, which he associated with being lazy.

During a winter day, the eagle may feed actively for an hour or so early in the morning and spend the next four or five hours sitting in a perch tree. If it's a nice day and the sun is shining, the birds may do a little soaring, but by mid- to late afternoon, they're usually headed for the roost.

The weather and activity level determine how much food the eagle needs. The colder the weather and the more active the animal is, the more food is required. Thus, by keeping activity levels to a minimum, the eagle can limit the amount of food it needs. In addition, during late winter, the eagles need to be putting on weight to carry them through migration and to help them prepare for breeding. Because of this, during the winter, easily attained food coupled with inactivity is essential.

Benjamin Franklin felt a bird that was so "lazy" that it just sat around and fed on dead animals would not be appropriate as our emblem. Others dis- agreed. They felt the majestic nature of the eagle and the ferocity with which it defended its home were admirable traits and as such represented the country.

With apologies to Mr. Franklin, the vulture-like activities of the eagles don't bother me in the least; in fact, it is that aspect of their natural history that intrigues me the most. The thing that separated the U.S. from the other nations of the world in 1776 was the great experiment in individual freedoms unknown in the history of the world, freedoms exemplified by the sight of a single bald eagle soaring over the river. Yet, in the winter, these fiercely territorial birds will put aside their natural aggression toward each other, group up, and benefit from that association. In a similar way, the independent colonies were able to put aside their distrust for each other and overcome their different national backgrounds so as to collect together into what has become the greatest nation this world has ever seen. Thus, in my mind, the eagle is a perfect symbol of the United States.

It's hard to concentrate when out on a night hike with two young boys. The task of keeping still and quiet along the river, while at the same time experiencing the excitement of the dark, was burdensome to them. It was time to go. I abandoned my thoughts of Ben Franklin and told Alex, my youngest, to lead us out to the pickup. He headed out through a thick stand of dogwood. Then it was through the numerous shallow side channels, some full, some not, and finally a maze of small cottonwoods until we emerged on the pasture near the pickup. I'm sure there were a number of shorter and easier routes to the truck, but none would have been as fun.

We shed our waders, coats, hats, and gloves and, like the eagles coming to the roost, the boys did battle to see who would get to sit up front. Once the pecking order was settled and Reece was situated next to me, Alex in the back, we headed out across the pastures of Jeffrey Island. It had been a great night hike: dark skies with bright shimmering stars, beavers slapping the water in alarm, the excitement of two young boys, and thirty-thee American bald eagles in the roost.

Chapter 15:
LEARNING THE FACTS OF LIFE…
THE HARD WAY!

In learning about the facts of life, you get a lot of help from your parents, grandparents, brothers, sisters, and friends. They all have stories for you, suggestions for you, and advice for you. The thing about the facts of life, however, is that you don't really learn about them until you have your own first experience with them. Take bees, for example.

I can't remember how I first learned about bees and their cousins, the wasps. I've stepped on them with bare feet, had them fly into the window of the pickup truck where they angrily lodged between me and the seat, and any number of times I've accidentally put a hand down on them. The most vivid memory I have, however, is of honey bees in clover along the edge of a hay field.

I was walking through the clover with my dog. Bees were everywhere, but I didn't worry about them. I live by the belief that if you leave bees and wasps alone, they will leave you alone. For most of my trip through the clover, they left me alone, and I left them alone. That is until one was drawn to the salty dampness of the back of my neck.

As we grow and age, we develop patterns of behavior called reflex actions. The value of a reflex is that your body reacts without first having to engage the brain. That makes the reaction much faster. One learned reflex action that I had acquired over the years was to slap mosquitoes and other bugs that land on me. Without thinking, reflex in control, I slapped the bee that had landed on my neck.

When you slap a bee, a chemical signal, known as an alarm pheromone, goes out from the injured bee to all the other bees in the area. I was instantly covered with bees. My body had never experienced a bee-coating, and so I had no reflex to deal with it. My brain had to figure out what was going on, and that took a few seconds. Apparently the bees were reacting by reflex because their response was instantaneous. That response consisted of stings on my ear, in my ear, just inside my nose, and on my eyelid and most of the bare skin of my neck, face, and arms.

The bees weren't too vindictive because they only followed me about fifty yards into the freshly cut hay where I was able to stop and evaluate the damage. My nose was running and my right eye was swelling shut, but for the most part, I wasn't in too bad of shape. My lesson learned, I headed back to the pickup where I assumed the dog, whose reaction time was much better than mine, would be waiting.

Great Uncle Otto learned a similar lesson. Every family has an Otto, the person who seems to have all the bad luck. As kids, Otto and his brothers would find the nests of ground-dwelling bumblebees. They would get brooms and stand around the hole in the ground. When a bee flew out they would kill it with the broom. The next bee would come out, and they would slap it, and so on until there were no more bees left (bumblebee hives have only a few individuals compared to a normal honey bee hive). Once the last bee was killed, the boys could dig up the nest and get to the "honey."

Uncle Otto decided to do a little honey gathering on his own one day. He made three mistakes. First, he missed that first bee. Now, honey bees typically only sting once, while wasps, hornets, and bumblebees have semi-automatic stingers that can sting more than once in rapid succession. That first bumblebee landed on Otto and fired. It was then Otto made his second mistake. He didn't just drop his broom and start running. Lastly, in his pain, he forgot about the bee hole and tried to slap the one stinging him. That allowed the second, third, fourth…well you get the idea. The entire nest of bees left the hole, one by one, and landed on Otto, one by one, and proceeded to rapid-fire sting. He then started to run, but it was way too late. Poor Uncle Otto swelled up like a balloon and was as sick as a dog for a week.

The stinger is the only protective mechanism bees and wasps have, but it is sufficient for the job! In the worker honeybee, the stinger is barbed and has a poison sac at the other end. When the bee inserts the stinger, it can get stuck due to the barbs and not be retracted. Thus when the bee pulls away, the stinger and poison sac are ripped from the abdomen of the bee. This is fatal to the bee.

Muscles along the stinger continue to contract for a time after being ripped from the bee. The contractions pump more and more poison down through the stinger and into the wound. Thus, if you do get stung, it is a good idea to try and get the stinger out as quickly as possible.

In the queen bee, there are no barbs on the stinger. They can sting over and over again; however, very few of us ever come in contact with queen bees. But as Uncle Otto found out, wasps and bumblebees, like the honey bee queen, have no barbs on their stingers. They can sting, release poison, withdraw the stinger, and stick it in again somewhere else, releasing more poison there.

Bee and wasp poisons contain various mixtures of chemicals that destroy tissues, cause pain, and stimulate our immune systems to react. Our immune reaction is complex and includes the release of histamines. These histamines cause swelling in the area of the sting. Swelling is a good thing because it is the result of fluids containing antibodies and other protective materials collecting at the site of the wound. These materials dilute the invading toxin, break down proteins that may make up the toxin, and prevent infection associated with the wound from spreading.

The problem that comes with swelling occurs when a person receives a large number of stings over much of their body. When that occurs, there is not only a lot of tissue damage, but there is also so much swelling the swelling itself can become dangerous. The swelling is somewhat temporary; however the damage from destroyed tissues can continue to cause problems for a few hours, days, or in Otto's case, weeks.

Some people, about 3–5% of the population, are so sensitive to the chemicals of the bee or wasp sting that a single sting will cause a body wide reaction called anaphylaxis. Anaphylaxis can cause severe illness and/or death if not treated quickly and correctly. In just about any given year in the United States, more people are hospitalized and/or die from bee stings (approximately 53 deaths/year) than from snake bites (approximately 6).

While not very many people die from a bee or wasp sting, most people have experienced it, and just about everyone can tell you about their experiences, experiences that painfully taught them something about the facts of natural history life. Alex, my youngest son, is no exception. He got one of his first lessons in the facts of life from an angry bumblebee.

I was putting together a collection of bees and wasps. There are over 4,000 different kinds of bees in the United States. There are carpenter bees, sweat bees, mason bees, cuckoo bees, bumblebees, and honey bees. Most of our bees are native species. The honey bee (*Apis mellifera*), the Nebraska State Insect (and state insect for 16 other states) is not. Honey bees have been imported from Europe and elsewhere since the 1600's.

While the products made from the honey and hives of honey bees are important, the true value of bees, in general, is their role in the pollination of just about every kind of flower we have in Nebraska.

I wanted as many of these different kinds of the native pollinators as I could get for the collection I was making, and so I spent a lot of time that summer out in the garden, catching bees. I placed them in a jar and added a ball of cotton soaked in fingernail polish remover (a bug poison readily available in my wife's medicine chest). Once dead, I pinned them out on a drying board and then later added them to the display case. The boys always liked to help collect stuff, so when Alex saw a nice big bumblebee buzzing from flower to flower, he didn't hesitate.

Bumblebees are native bees, and there are about 45 or so different kinds in the U.S., with about 20 found in Nebraska. Most are ground nesters. Typically a bumblebee hive consists of a queen and one generation of workers, anywhere from 20 to 200 individuals. There are four species of cuckoo bumblebees in the mix of 20. These are bees that mate, invade the nest of another bumblebee, and kill the queen. The invader then lays her eggs. The "workers" don't know the difference between their queen and the invading queen, and so they feed and raise the cuckoo bumblebee larvae. Cuckoos are birds that lay their eggs in the nests of other birds so as to let those birds raise the chicks, hence the name for the bumblebee.

Bees as a whole are in trouble. For us, these insects may well be some of the most important animals on earth, and so this is a concern. As much as 30–40% of plants that provide us with "food" depend upon the pollination by bees in order to make seeds and/or fruit. Then if you consider things like alfalfa, a plant important in the meat industry, our food dependence upon bees may be as high as 50%. Bumblebees are no exception. Like so many animals, the habitats for bees and bumblebees (mostly wildflowers) are diminishing. This has led to multiple proposals to list species of bumblebees as "threatened and/or endangered" under the federal and state Endangered Species Lists. This past year, the rusty-patched bumblebee. *Bombus affinis*, a species not found in Nebraska but north and east of here, was added to the federal T&E list. Here in Nebraska, we have the western bumblebee (true to its name, out in the Panhandle) and the yellow-banded bumblebee (northern edge) that are being considered for addition to the list.

The bumblebee Alex saw had the scientific name of *Bombus bimaulatus*, or the two-spot bumble bee. At the time, he knew nothing about the facts of life as they pertained to *Bombus bimaulatus*. He ran over to the bee and gently grabbed the fuzzy yellow and black insect in a two-year old grip.

Kids learn lessons every day. They have piano lessons, spelling lessons, language lessons, and they have life lessons. When you learn a lesson, I mean really learn it, you don't ever forget it. We had warned Alex a number of times about bees and wasps. We told him they would sting him. We told him it would hurt. However, two-year-olds don't listen to Mom and Dad's warnings about bees any better than 26-year-olds do about motorcycles, so those warnings went unheeded. Unheeded, that is, until that afternoon 24 years ago when he was taught a very personal fact of life by a bumble bee. A fact he has never forgotten!

Chapter 16:

SKUNK SNAKES

"Wow…that thing stinks!" Jay exclaimed as I dragged the skunk snake out from under the washing machine. He backed up a step as I stood with the wiggling reptile in my hands. Jay doesn't like snakes. No, that's not correct. Jay hates snakes. He can't stand them when he's camping, hiking, hunting, or at baseball practice, and he sure can't stand them in his washroom. However, like other serpent-phobics (snake haters), he is intrigued by them and will gladly take a closer look, if I have them securely in my hands, as this one was.

Usually Jay's answer to a snake is to chop its head off with a spade, blow it up with the 12 gauge, or harvest it with the mower. But, because none of these options were available to him in his wife's laundry room, he called me. He told me his wife saw a big snake crawl under the washing machine. Both his wife and Jay were correct. It was a big one, and the darn thing did stink. We have fox snakes, bull snakes, and rat snakes, but this was what I like to call a "skunk" snake. Google it, and you will get nothing because this is a name I use. The actual name of the snake is garter snake.

Garter snakes are Nebraska's most common snake. They are found from one end of the state to the other. In fact, we have four different kinds of snakes that rightfully could be called garter snakes. These are the western terrestrial garter snake, found, as its name suggests, in western Nebraska. Along the east edge of the state, also living up to its name, is the eastern ribbon snake. Across the entire state are the common garter snake (also called the red-sided garter snake), and the Plains garter snake. The intruder in Jay's washroom was a large pregnant female Plains garter snake.

The Plains garter snake is also true to its name as it is found throughout the Great Plains from Texas into the providence's of Canada. Here in Nebraska, it is more common than the common garter snake, though the common garter snake is pretty common. Confused? That's the problem with common names (no pun intended). They may make sense in one location, but not in another. Because of that, biologists use a standard name, a scientific name, a Latin name.

All of the true garter snakes belong to the group *Thamnophis*, and they all have specific, or species names. Take, for example, the eastern ribbon snake. In Missouri, they call it the western ribbon snake. Biologists the world-over call it *Thamnophis proximus*.

Garter snakes are semi-aquatic. They feed on frogs, toads, fish, and worms and will even eat things they find dead and partially decayed. They will also eat eggs, small mammals, and baby birds, and I once kept one as a pet that ate other snakes.

Without question, garter snakes are the most common, most widespread, and most abundant snakes in both Nebraska and the rest of United States (where there are about 13 different species). They all have 1–3 stripes that run the length of the body (many times the stripes will be somewhat yellow) with a checkerboard pattern of red, orange, yellow, or black located between the strip that runs down the back and the ones on the sides. It's the strips and checkerboard pattern that allow you to identify the various kinds.

Because of their diet, you generally find garter snakes near water. It might be a pond, stream, river, or a well-watered vegetable garden. In fact, may people think they are *garden* snakes, not *garter* snakes. Again, common names confuse. They could rightfully be garden snakes; they are in the garden. They were called garter snakes because at one time men wore garters to hold up their socks. The garters were usually striped in a way similar to the snakes. No matter; to scientists they're *Thamnophis*.

All of our North American garters are more-or-less harmless; however that doesn't hold true for the entire world. In Africa, the "common garter snake" is a deadly poisonous one. Again…a problem with the name.

The Plains garter snake (known to biologist as *Thamnophis radix*) and the common garter snake (*Thamnophis sirtalis*) live throughout the state, but you don't necessarily find them in the same place. *T. radix* is usually found in more open grasslands. They are what you would expect to find in town, in your yard, and in the garden. *T. sirtalis* patrols the banks of rivers, lakes, and ponds. *T.*

radix feeds on insects, worms, and the common (there's that word again) garden toad. (Actually, throughout most of Nebraska, the most common toad is the Woodhouse's toad, or to biologists, *Bufo woodhousei*, though that name has recently been changed to *Anaxyrus woodhousei*.) *T. sirtalis*, living along the various bodies of water, probably feed more on frogs and fish, though they too will snarf up a worm or toad if the opportunity presents itself.

Both species, like other garter snakes, bear their young alive. Live birth in reptiles is not the same as live birth in mammals. In mammals, a placenta connects the developing embryo to the mother. Nutrients are exchanged throughout the entire gestation (pregnancy). In reptiles, an egg is produced. That egg contains a yolk similar to birds and other egg-laying animals. The only difference is that the egg doesn't have a shell and isn't laid. These eggs are retained in the body of the mother snake. No nutrients are exchanged. When the young snakes are developed, they "hatch" and are "born."

In both species, mating occurs in the spring almost immediately upon emergence from their hibernation den. In some species, large balls of snakes made up of one female and as many as twenty or thirty males can be found. The males are all competing with each other, attempting to be the one that mates with the single female.

After mating, the snakes all head out for the summer. It is believed the snakes leave behind trails of sent they then follow back to the den in the fall. The young snakes develop inside the mother until late August or early September at which time up to 70 can be born. In the many snakes I've kept, the most a single snake ever produced was 37. The snake at Jay's house was a large pregnant female. Neither Jay nor his wife was very happy to hear that she had the potential to add another 30–70 little snakes to their basement!

Garter snakes are medium in size for snakes. Both of the common species here in Nebraska grow to about three feet, and one has been collected and is preserved in the University of Nebraska collection that exceeded four feet. The female (as in many reptile species) is larger than the male. Quite a bit larger.

Garter snakes have four mechanisms for protection. First and foremost is to hide. With their striped appearance, they blend in very well in the tall grasses and sedges of a wetland. If they are disturbed, they can move quite rapidly. The long, thin shape coupled with the strips makes them deceptively quick.

If camouflage or flight doesn't work, they can be very aggressive, and they will bite. The bite isn't dangerous; however allergic reactions to some kinds of garter snakes have been reported. The bite of any and all snakes does present a problem. Snakes have a number of razor sharp teeth that are all pointed toward the back of the snake's throat. When the snake bites, if you are like me, your first reaction is to jerk your hand back. The many teeth leave a series of scratches on your hand. The scratches can easily become infected.

The last line of defense for the snake comes when you pick them up. Garter snakes will empty themselves, either by regurgitating or defecating all over the place. (You've heard of the fight or flight reaction. Well, I call this the puke or poop reaction!) In addition, like a skunk, they will spray into the air, on your hand, out into Jay's washroom, etc. the foul smelling contents of their anal glands. This smell is very distinctive, very unpleasant, and the one Jay had commented on when I pulled his laundry room snake from under the washing machine. This smell can also be used against the snake as my son, Alex, discovered. He trained our retriever to hunt up and retrieve garter snakes. The two of them caught 29 snakes in our empty lot in less than an hour.

We have a den located on our property as well as a place where Plains garter snakes just love to hang out. The "hangout" is under the boards of a pile of junk that Cindy, my wife, wants me to clean up. Cindy, while not quite the snake-phobic that Jay is, still doesn't see any reason to keep a pile of junk around just to attract a bunch of snakes. However, the boys and I like it, so it remains. I carried the snake I found under Jay's washing machine out to the pickup, and told him I would take it to the "hangout" and release it there. He was relieved. He figured that would be the end to this large, pregnant snake. I didn't tell him that garter snakes have been known to return to a den site from as far away as three miles or that the young can track the adults so as to locate the site. No, there are some things about these striped little skunk snakes that it might be best if Jay didn't know.

Chapter 17:
BARN OWLS

I just "handed off" three young barn owls to Connie, who also lives in Gothenburg and is a Relay Team Volunteer with Raptor Recovery Nebraska. She was willing to put aside her daily activities to get the birds to Audubon's Rowe Sanctuary near Gibbon. That saved me either taking the birds myself or from being tempted to care for the darn things.

Years ago, I took up the responsibility of raising a young owl, and from that experience I learned a valuable lesion. At the time I was teaching in Ewing, Nebraska, and one of my students brought in a very young great horned owl. We (my students and I) decided to "raise" the owl in the classroom.

The first thing on the agenda was to name the bird. My seniors and I took the bird to the kindergarten class to show them the owl, and we decided they could name her. They thought "Barney" was a good name for a barn owl. I explained that Barney was fine, except this was a great horned owl, not a barn owl. Well, you guessed it. The owl was promptly named Horny, much to my senior students' delight.

Horny did provide for some lively entertainment in the classroom. She lived on top of the microscope cabinet. When she had to relieve herself, she would back up and drop her…dropping…over the edge. The first time she did that, it landed smack in the middle of the seat of one of the desks. Fortunately, Gina, who was sitting there that hour, was up sharpening her pencil at the time. Needless to say, she demanded a change in seating.

Gina's sister Sandy wasn't quite as lucky. As Horny grew, we taught her to fly. One day, Sandy was sitting in her desk, located across the room from the cabinet, brushing her hair. Horny must have taken the brush for a tasty morsel as the next thing we all knew she launched off the top of the cabinet and landed, talons first, on Sandy's head. It was time for Horny to be set free.

Horny didn't want to be set free. She had imprinted on me, and as far as she was concerned, we were mates. I already had a mate, one of the human persuasion, and I had no interest in forming a second relationship with an owl. I had Rita, the student who had brought the owl in, take the owl back to the farmyard where she had found it. Horny didn't live through the month. She would beg at the back door of the farmhouse, and one day they found her there, dead. My lesson? If you don't know what you are doing, you shouldn't try and rehabilitate a wild animal! Fortunately, a second lesson, that I didn't learn the hard way, is that it was illegal for us to try. Owls, along with just about every species of bird found in Nebraska, are protected by law, and you must have special permits, both state and federal, to keep them in captivity. I don't have those permits. Connie and the other volunteers with Raptor Recovery Nebraska do have the permits.

Pat, a canal patrolman for the Central Nebraska Public Power and Irrigation District, found the young barn owls along the canal. The birds had been in a cavity in a cut-bank along the road, and the bank had sloughed off sometime in the night. Pat picked them off the road the next morning and brought them to me. I then turned them over to Connie.

There are about 130 different species of owls worldwide with barn owls being the most widely distributed. Here in Nebraska, we have nine different species that either nest or winter here. The barn owl, along with the great horned owl and the short-eared owl, are found throughout the state. The other owls—long-eared, screech, northern saw-whet, barred, and burrowing—are found only in special habitats, and the snowy owl occasionally migrates this far south during the winter.

Barn owls go hand in hand with agriculture. They use the rafters and lofts of barns (hence the name) and old buildings, silos, and grain bins for roosting and nesting. At night, they glide silently along the edges of fields and fencerows, picking off unwary mice and other rodents.

The number of rodents a family of barn owls will eat is amazing. According to information available from the Nebraska Game and Parks Commission, one pair of barn owls were observed bringing 21 rodents to a nest in 25 minutes!

Below a roost or nest, you will find large numbers of owl pellets. When an owl eats, it swallows its prey whole. The bones, fur, or feathers cannot be digested, and the stomach of the owl packs them into a tight pellet that is then regurgitated. By tearing apart the pellets, you can determine what the owls have been eating.

Barn owls have large families. They lay from 4–11 eggs. Usually there are two or three days between the laying of each egg, which means the first egg may hatch as much as a month before the last egg. If there is plenty of food, this is not a problem. However, if food is in short supply, the younger owls may be driven from the nest by their hungry, larger, and older siblings, or they even may be used as "lunch."

Barn owl eggs hatch after about 31 days of incubation, and the young birds are able to fly eight weeks later. The adults continue to feed the young for about four more weeks, even though the young are able to fly.

Barn owls don't live very long. Two or three years in the wild is normal. Despite the short lives of individual birds, a nest area may be used year after year. I know of a rocky ledge at Lake McConaughy in Keith County, Nebraska that has supported barn owls for at least 26 years. Below that rocky ledge are layers upon layers of the bones of the hapless gophers and mice that have fed as many as ten generations of owls.

Owls, and specifically barn owls, are the most efficient of all bird hunters. Their eyes and ears are specially adapted to the dark and to finding prey. Their eyes are fixed in the head and face forward. This gives the birds binocular vision, which is crucial as it gives them depth perception. The ears also have a "depth perception"-like structure. Binocular vision means that both eyes see the same object, but from slightly different angles. This allows the brain to estimate the distance to the object based upon those angles. With owls, the ears are also aligned in an asymmetric way such that a sound will reach each ear at slightly different times. This allows the bird to estimate the distance and direction to the sound in the same way that the eyes do an object. In lab tests, barn owls have successfully captured small mice in rooms with virtually no light available.

Barn owl numbers have diminished. This is due, in large part, to the cleaning of old fencerows and the use of pesticides for rodent control. However, the biggest impact may well be the loss of nesting sites. Old houses, silos, barns, and sheds with open attics are becoming rare throughout the state. In talking with Connie, she indicated that the recovery members are seeing an impact of the loss of those old nest sites.

This year, according to Connie, a number of young barn owls have been brought in. As farmers get ready to deliver storage corn, they find the birds actually nesting in the corn at the top of the bin. The farmers really don't like the mess of partially eaten mice, pellets, and droppings in their corn. The value of having a family of barn owls around the farm, eating hundreds of mice and rats is attractive to the farmers, however, they obviously would prefer the birds nest somewhere other than in the corn bins.

The rehabilitators have been suggesting nest boxes for the owl. It may take a few years, but, if barn owls take over a nest box, there is satisfaction in having provided a place for them as well as in the knowledge that you now have mousers better than any cat that has ever lived. But, if any young owls fall from the nest box, either put them back or call Connie because not only is it work raising them, they fall in love at the drop of a mouse…and that can be a little disquieting when the owl's name is Horny.

Chapter 18:

ALEX'S SNAKE

My youngest boy isn't afraid of spiders or snakes. For his entire life, there have been spiders in aquariums in the basement or snakes in cages in the dog pen. We've watched funnel web spiders in the garden over the course of a summer and have any number of small garter snakes in the back yard. I view this lack of fear as a good thing; however, there are times when a little more fear is warranted.

A few years ago, we were spending a late summer weekend at Lake Mc-Conaughy. Cindy and I took our morning coffee to the beach, and the boys went exploring. It was a cool, breezy morning. Too cool for swimming.

The boys were about a 100 yards up the beach when they started yelling at me: "Dad, a snake!"

We were on the Sandhills side of the lake, so I assumed it was a garter snake or bull snake.

"It's a rattlesnake, Dad," my youngest son, Alex, yelled.

That settled it in my mind. A bull snake. Rattlesnakes are found at the Lake, but more often on the south side than the north where we were. Also, rattlesnakes and bull snakes look a little bit alike, and knowing how excited the boys were, I was sure they were mistaken in their identification of the snake. I needed a bull snake because the local Cub Scouts had asked me to give a presentation on spiders and snakes. I put my coffee down and headed up the beach to catch the snake.

When I got there, I discovered that my hunch was wrong and that Alex's identification of the snake was correct. There, coiled on the beach at the edge of the water, was a three-foot-long prairie rattlesnake.

"I thought it was a bull snake, Dad," Alex said, "and I tried to pick it up. When I touched it, it started to rattle its tail, and its head came up like this." He used his arm and hand to show how the snake had coiled into striking position.

I found a piece of driftwood and pinned the snake's head to the sand. The cool of the morning prevented the snake from moving very quickly, and that made pinning it fairly easy. The slowness of the snake had also protected Alex in his attempt to pick it up.

With the head pinned, I was able to get a good hold on its neck, and I carried it back to the campground, explaining to the boys along the way that they should never touch or try to pick up any snake until they were sure, absolutely sure, of what kind of snake it was.

When we got back to Cindy and Alex related his adventure in grabbing a live rattlesnake, the lecture began again, this time from his mother. We went up to our campsite, and I took a small hammer, put the snake on the hard road, and thumped it in the head. Normally I wouldn't have killed the snake, but since we were in a public campground I didn't want to leave it there where it might bite some child, nor did I have anything secure enough, in Cindy's opinion, to put it in so as to carry it out alive. Also, Alex wanted to make a hatband from its hide.

After breakfast, we broke camp, packed up all the gear, and headed home. The entire way Alex talked of his rattlesnake adventure and Cindy scolded him for touching the snake. Listening to the telling and scolding, I got to thinking about the similarity between bull snakes, rattlesnakes, and a third snake common on the prairies of Nebraska, the hognose snake.

In nature, there are innumerable examples of animals resembling other animals. Sometimes it's because the two animals are closely related. That isn't the case with the three snakes I had in mind. The three are not at all closely related.

In biology, we group things according to similarities. For example, all things that are multicellular, move, and eat other things are grouped in the Animal Kingdom. Those animals that for a time during their lives have a dorsal nerve cord with a supportive structure are grouped into the Phylum Chordata. That includes animals with backbones. The Phylum is then further divided into Classes: fishes, birds, mammals, and in this case, the Class Reptilia.

The Class Reptilia is then divided into orders with snakes belonging to the Order Squamata. Orders are further divided into Families. The bull snake and hognose snakes belong to the family Colubridae, while the rattlesnake belongs to the family Viperidae.

Rattlesnakes have hollow fangs in the front of the mouth, something none of the snakes in the family Colubridae have. Those fangs are much larger than the other teeth and fold up when the snake closes its mouth. Bull snakes and hognose snakes have a lot of teeth, however none are hollow, and they are all pretty much the same size.

Rattlesnakes bear their young alive. It is different from the kind of live birth in mammals. In live-bearing snakes, there is only limited direct connection between the mother snake and the young during development. The embryos are contained within eggs with yolk for food. The eggs are not laid but are kept within the body of the mother throughout development. Once developed, the young snakes sort of hatch from the eggs and are then born. Bull snakes and hognose snakes lay their eggs. These eggs have tough, leathery shells, and once the eggs have been deposited, they are on their own to hatch sometime later.

Families are further divided into genetic groups called Genus. The Genus of the bull snake is *Pituophis* while that of the hog nose snake is *Heterodon* (in biology we always underline or type in italics the Genus name). The differences in these two snakes are also significant. The bull snake is a constrictor that suffocates its prey before eating it. The saliva of the hognose snakes is a mild poison that helps to subdue their prey so it can be swallowed alive. The hognose does have slightly larger teeth at the back of the mouth that may cause deeper wounds in the prey, allowing the poison to penetrate better. Bull snakes have no poison and have teeth of uniform size.

So, if it isn't the genetic similarity between these snakes that account for their similar appearance, what is it? The similarity between the snakes is due to their protective coloration.

Protective coloration in animals has been divided by biologists into four categories. One category is mimicry. This is when one animal does look like another and that similarity in appearance is an advantage. An example would be flies that look like bees. Most animals know from experience that bees sting, thus they tend to leave them alone. Flies that look like bees are also left alone.

Another example, and the classic one given, is that of the Viceroy and Monarch butterflies. These two species look very, very much alike. The Monarch, as a caterpillar, feeds on milkweeds. Milkweeds are somewhat poisonous, and it is believed that when the butterfly undergoes metamorphosis into the adult form, those poisons make it taste awful. Birds that try and eat the Monarchs don't like them and thus leave them alone from then on. Viceroy butterflies don't feed on milkweeds, and I presume they taste just fine. However, birds that can't tell the difference between the two species don't know that and leave them alone as well.

A second category is known as warning coloration. These are animals with bright colors, usually bright red, orange, or yellow. Examples are bees and wasps (and of course the flies that mimic them). A bird that tries to eat a bee or wasp will get stung. It will recognize the bright colors of the stinging insect and never again try to eat something colored that way.

The third category is cryptic coloration. This is when the animal has the same basic color as its background, red-bellied snakes for example. These are small snakes that are the exact color of dead grass. They blend in with their background so well that, unless you are out specifically looking for them, you will probably never see them.

Rattlesnakes, bull snakes, and hognose snakes all employ cryptic coloration to a degree, but in addition, they also employ the fourth category of protective coloration: disruptive coloration. With disruptive coloration, there are blotches and strips of light and dark hue that produce a lighted and shadowed effect on the animal. This helps to break up the outline of the animal in the exact way camouflage clothing breaks up the outline of the hunter. Without an outline, the snake becomes effectively invisible.

The disruptive coloration would be useless if the colors were not somewhat drab and similar to the coloration of the surrounding habitat (cryptic coloration), and so it is that all three snakes have blotches and stripes of gray and black coloration that hides them in the grass. The blotches and stripes of gray and black also makes them look a lot alike, and thus identifying them is a problem for young boys like Alex.

At times, the snakes also behave in similar ways, and that can be confusing. But, like the coloration, the behavior isn't some attempt to copy each other; it's simply a protective action that most snakes perform. For example, most snakes vibrate their tails when excited. In the rattlesnakes, this makes the warning noise we all associate with them. In the bull snakes and others, the tail may stir dead leaves and grass, also making a noise that to some may be mistaken for the rattle of the "buzztails." Harmless snakes hiss and coil up in a position to strike and bite at anything they perceive as a danger. Hognose snakes also spread their heads, which makes them look bigger, and that may provide further protection. This habit has given them the common name of "spread head" or "puff adder." However, this aggression and the larger head of the hognose also fool people into believing the snake is poisonous and thus harmful.

There are four kinds of poisonous snakes in Nebraska, the copperhead and three different kinds of rattlesnake. Along with those, there are about 40 other kinds of snakes that are not dangerous. Though harmless, many like the bull snake and hognose snake, look or act like the poisonous ones, and thus the fear of snakes many people have is not necessarily a bad thing. In fact, a little more fear of snakes by my youngest would be a good thing.

Chapter 19:

TURTLES, LIZARDS, AND GOOD SCIENCE

Reptiles are popular in the pet industry. They are popular both with the individuals that buy the things as well as with those who sell them. Those who do the buying like the exotic nature of the beasts and the fact that most people don't have cold-blooded pets. The sellers like it because so many of the buyers have no idea what kind of reptile it is they are buying, so the sellers can call it just about anything.

A case in point, actually two cases: A few years ago I was called by an elementary teacher and asked to come into her classroom and identify some small white "bugs" that were hopping all over an aquarium in which the class turtle was kept. It turns out the "bugs" were springtails, and we assumed they had hatched from eggs laid in the wood-shaving bedding the teacher had purchased.

Relieved that the small white "crawlies" weren't lice or fleas, she began to tell me about her "African Red-Legged Tortoise." I explained to her that the turtle wasn't from Africa, wasn't a tortoise, and that if she had a female instead of a male, it wouldn't even have had red legs. What she had, at a price tag of $29.98 (which included the small aquarium and bedding), was an Ornate Box Turtle, sometimes in Nebraska called a sand turtle.

How disappointing for her to discover that her exotic African Tortoise was actually a small turtle she could have collected for free in just about any pasture located near town. Heck, I could have given her one as I had two living in the dog pen at that time.

The store clerk sold her the turtle, aquarium, bedding—the whole thing— because she thought she was getting some sort of exotic pet that would make her class unique. She thought having this strange creature from Africa would stimulate the curiosity and imagination of her students. I told her the class was still unique as no other teacher in school had turtles. One teacher had hamsters, the biology teacher had a bird, and the FFA students were growing shrimp, but this was the only class in school with a reptile. I also pointed out that it would be the turtle, not where the turtle came from, that would be of interest to the students.

Too often, people think that some animal from a remote location miles and miles from the prairies of Nebraska will be more exciting and entertaining than one from around here. They also feel, somehow, that we can learn more from the exotic animal than from one collected locally.

The second case in point: Walking through the pet section of the local nursery store a couple of years ago I saw an aquarium that contained some lizards, including one of my favorites, a six-lined racerunner.

Written on the side of the glass was a list of the lizards and their cost. I was curious what a racerunner was worth as they are not the easiest to catch, but it wasn't listed. A young man working in the store told me the lizard with the long tail was a "striped iguana" and the cost was $9.79.

Well, racerunners do have stripes (and one sub-species of six-lined racerunner actually has seven stripes), but they are not iguanas. Iguana is the general name for a family of lizards that live mostly in the New World. The large green vegetarian lizards often used in "dinosaur" movies are the kind most people recognize as iguanas, however, racerunners are not of that family.

Here in Nebraska, we do have four different kinds of lizards that rightfully could be called iguanas as they belong to that family. Two of the four are fence lizards (eastern fence lizard and the sagebrush lizard), a third is the lesser earless lizard, and we have one kind of "horned toad" or short-horned lizard. Along with these iguanas, we have other kinds of lizards as well.

We have at least four different kinds of lizards that belong to the skink family. Skinks are slim, quick, and somewhat shiny lizards that live along rivers, streams, and lakes. Lastly, we have one kind of whiptail (the six-lined racerunner), the lizard that the store was selling as the striped iguana.

Racerunners are found throughout the state but are most common in drier habitats with short vegetation and sandy, loose soil. They are either male or female. You may think that sounds silly, that all animals are either male or female, but that is not the case in some species of racerunners. For example, there are no male New Mexico Racerunners only females. In this species, fertile eggs are produced by each and every individual lizard, without mating, and the eggs all hatch into more females. Our Nebraska variety however, being male or female, must first mate in order to produce offspring. They do so in May with the female laying the eggs in June. Usually the eggs are deposited in a hole or tunnel underground and they incubate there for 50–60 days with the young emerging in August.

Racerunners are up to 3.5 inches in length, not counting their tail, which may be another 3–4 inches, and they are well named. They are the fastest reptiles found in Nebraska, and they have been clocked at up to 18 mph. This speed allows them to catch a variety of insects and gives them an advantage in escaping the many predators that feed on things like small lizards and snakes.

The long tail of the racerunner is another adaptation that aids it in escape. One function of the tail is common throughout many species of lizards. The tail has a weak point at its base. If you grab the tail, it will break off, separating from the body at the weak point. The tail, once separated from the rest of the lizard, whips back and forth. If a bird or small snake breaks the tail, this movement attracts the attention of the predator, allowing the lizard to make its escape.

The tail also has a role in the speed achievable by racerunners and other whiptails. Some students at the University of Nebraska, under the guidance of Dr. Royce Ballinger, once tested the impact of losing its tail on the speed of a racerunner.

They first caught a bunch of racerunners complete with their tails. (And from someone who has chased these lizards a great deal, let me assure you that that in of itself was no simple task!) Next they built a special lizard "raceway," and they ran the lizards down this raceway, timing them and calculating their speed.

Once they had an "average" speed for the whole group of lizards, they broke the tails off the lizards and ran them again. Without their tails, the lizards ran 36% slower than they did when the tail was complete.

Apparently, the tail gives the lizard balance and stability, which in turn enables the lizard to run faster. Is there any practical value to knowing that six-lined racerunners are able to run 18 miles per hour with a tail and only 12 miles per hour without? I don't know. Maybe that knowledge will be of value to someone designing stabilizers for boats and planes, but that's not why the students did the study. The study was to answer a simple question; that being, is a long tail of any advantage to the lizard other than as a decoy allowing the lizard to escape when a predator strikes? It turns out that, yes, a long tail does have a value other than simply as a decoy.

So of what value to us is the knowledge that a long tail makes lizards run faster? There are two values. First is that we have learned another piece of information about the natural world in which we live. It's a small piece to be sure, but the more we learn about our world, both the large and small, the better off we are. The second value derived from this study has little to do with the speed that lizards run. The value is in what the students had to do in order to determine the speed that lizards run. It was the process of isolating a single variable (length of the tail) and then the designing of a test to determine the impact a change in that variable will have on the problem as a whole (how fast can a lizard run). It's this process, the thought process and design process, that lies at the root of what we call good science.

From second graders to graduate students, Nebraska has all it takes to make the learning about natural history exciting, challenging, and just plain fun. Besides, good science can be done equally well, if not better, with ornate box turtles and six-lined racerunners as with any animal from some distant land because good science isn't about what you are studying, it's all about how you carry out the study.

Chapter 20:

CRANE MUSIC

Crane Music. It means different things to different people. To the sportsman in Texas, it represents the winter. Hunting season. Blinds set out in cornfields, decoys, and calls to entice the birds within range. Bag and possession limits. New shotguns, old stories, and the never-ending question as to how to cook up a crane.

To the crane-viewing host in Nebraska, the music means time and money. Time spent meeting with people each and every morning to take them, in the dark, to the blind. Coffee and questions. Then again that evening, more people to the blinds. More questions. Questions answered and cranes watched and heard at twenty-five dollars a person. Twenty-five dollars, the cost of being close to the roost, hearing the noise, and watching the last minute adjustment of wings as thousands of birds jockey for position in the shallows of the river. Twenty-five dollars: money to fund conservation activities. A bargain to most.

To an old bird watcher, mostly retired, in his 45th year of hearing "those of the gray wing," it's a return to younger days. Days filled with the excitement of personal discovery. Days filled with the learning about new animals, new birds, and new sounds. There were no blinds then. He'd ask a farmer's permission and then crawl through the tall, wet river grass to a place where he could watch and listen to the birds coming to roost. The answer from the farmer was always yes, and the experience was always rewarding.

The music now means a crowd where once there were but a few. Where once he struggled to inform the people, he now struggles to see past their gathered bodies with their bulky and expensive camera equipment. The music of the cranes brings a nostalgic desire for those nights spent alone on the banks of the river watching and listening, a time alone, but not lonely.

To the landowner, the sound of the cranes means getting the fields ready for the spring planting. It is also the sound of calving season. Late night rides through rough riverside pastures searching for the young heifer struggling with her first calf. The music of the crane is the music of the midwife. The drying of calves in the warmth of the porch and the sadness of one not saved.

The music of the cranes also brings with it the annoyance of the crane watchers, crane watchers from out of town, out of state, some from out of the country, who park along the roads making travel with wide farm equipment difficult, ephemeral members of the community who take up the roads, crowd the bridges at dusk, and a few who are trespassers coming onto the land without asking.

The crane watchers are an annoyance, soon to be gone, but the music brings with it a fear that persists. A fear of losing more than a calf. A fear the endangered label, which belongs on a different bird, a different crane, one with a different song, will make life on the river-farm harder. He fears the presence of this crane. He fears it will limit his use of water for irrigating his crops, and so he attends meetings where the people of the river ask questions and express concerns. The music of the crane brings uneasiness.

To the crane watcher, the music is a symphony of wonder. A sound so different, yet one that resonates within. A song remembered through some genetic tie with yesteryear. The crane watcher also hears the call of those worried for the crane. He also attends meetings. Meetings where the talk is of the destruction and loss of habitat. Talks of extirpation and extinction. Of forest and sand and changes in the flows of the river. The music of the crane is to them, the cry of alarm.

And through it all the music continues. The cranes know nothing about calves and conservation. They are not aware of the people-filled blinds and the popcorn-like sounds of the camera shutters preserving their flights, roosts, and ancient dances. They know nothing of the conflict between the watcher and landowner, nor do they care. They also know nothing and care nothing about the biologist who sits alone in the dark, listening to the evening's performance. The music continues, and last night, a cold night during the final week of March, it continued for me, that biologist.

For me, the music of the crane is the call to camp. To drive the 45 minutes in from the main gate to a grassy area between the river trees and the pasture plums. A short hike, and then a crawl to my chosen observation point. Then, as the old birdwatcher used to do, I sit alone on the bank in the wonderful darkness of the star-filled Nebraska night and listened to endless calls of the shadows out in the river.

Cold and stiff from the time spent motionless along the river, I crawled back to my camp. A quick cold supper of old pizza and then off to sleep in my sleeping bag placed out on the open grass, a sleep interrupted by the continuing symphony, a sleep that ended in a frost covered sunrise.

Now awake, I hesitate to leave the warmth of the bag. Digging my journal from my pack, I place within this entry that documents my night, documentation of the fact that the cranes, about 8,000 as best as I could tell, used this stretch of river last night, documentation that I, too, was here.

Documentation not needed by the cranes. Just as they don't care if we watch from the blinds, camera's clicking away, with twenty dollar bills exchanged, they don't care that I record their presence. But I care and others care. People, unlike cranes, strive to document presence. Are they there? Were they there? Will they be there tomorrow? Presence, and thus absence, is important to us.

Cranes have had a presence along the Platte for as long as there has been a Platte. And, to you and me, the Platte has been here a long, long time. To the birds, not so long. The age of this species, or at least one very close in the visual appearance documented by fossil remains, is numbered in the millions. The age of the Platte, documented in geological record, is in the thousands.

Long before there was a Platte River, there were cranes, cranes that fed and roosted elsewhere. Even after the river expressed its presence, it is doubtful the birds used the Platte as much then—whenever "then" was—as they do now. The cranes of today, the cranes of the Platte, eat corn, corn produced in staggering amounts along the Platte.

Corn is a wonderful food. It contains sugars and oils that provide the highest quantity and quality of nutrients for the cranes. To the crane, corn is a better food than the roots and tubers they had to dig for in times gone by. Corn is easier to come by, richer in nutrients, and far more plentiful. True, the cornfields have replaced wetlands, which provided a greater variety of foods, specifically those that provide protein. Protein is important, but it isn't protein the birds need at this time. What are needed are calories. Fats and oils. Weight gain for reproduction. As any marathon runner can tell you, these birds are into carbohydrate loading for the long "run" to their breeding grounds. They need complicated carbs. Corn. Thus, the cranes stop in the Platte valley for a few weeks to fatten up on the abundant corn supply available here before they spiral upward to catch the south winds to their arctic nesting grounds.

Unfortunately for the young naturalist, no longer does the landowner welcome him, granting him permission to make the quiet trek to the water's edge in the dark of a spring evening. In addition, the conservation groups and government agencies discourage the closeness that comes from such a trek. With the gain in the number of cranes using the Platte River along with the gain in the number of people watching the cranes has come a loss. More and more to protect nature, we are required to isolate people from it. This is sad.

To paraphrase Edward Abbey, the secrets and love for nature cannot be learned through talks and lectures, articles and essays. Nor can it be learned through the finest of photographs, videos, and interactive computer simulation. Nature can only truly be learned through first-hand experiences like crawling through the dew-wet grasses of the Platte River on a cold spring evening, sandburs in hand, knee, and elbows, to listen to the call of an ancient bird.

Then, cold, wet, blood on cheek, sandbur in hand, and sitting in the dark, there is a chance you might learn something, something of value. But there is no guarantee. The only guarantee is that you will be out of the blind, away from the crowd, alone, but not lonely. More importantly, you will be in a position to at least watch the birds and hear their music unfiltered by the thoughts and opinions of others. You'll be in a position to determine for yourself the value of the cranes and their music.

POSTSCRIPT

I come from the semi-arid region of Nebraska where things that we called rivers are actually small, clay-filled streams. I then moved and lived along the banks of the Elkhorn River. People from other states would say this is still a small stream, but to me it opened a door to a biology that I had never experienced.

I took to both studying the river and playing in it. That led me to another river, the Niobrara. The Niobrara is my favorite river, followed closely by the Dismal. For years we canoed both rivers.

I moved yet again. This time to the banks of the Platte River, the River that more than any other identifies Nebraska and more than any other shaped my subsequent life, a river whose history, both human and natural, is extensive, and I love both. So I end this small booklet with a look at "my" river.

WALKING THE RIVER

Have you ever taken a walk in a river? Not just any river, but a prairie river. A wide, shallow ribbon of water carrying the remains of granite mountains across a flatland topography. A river that can't seem to make up its mind. A left turn here, a right turn there. Doubling back on itself as if to return the rocks back to their birth-site, only to reconsider and double back again to its original heading. A river that gets wide and shallow, sluggish and warm, then narrows to a current with force and vitality...only to widen once more.

A river that chooses first one channel and then another, abandoning the first to be overgrown, choked, and crowded with vegetation. Then in a month, a year, a century, the water returns to claim its original path.

A walk in this river stirs and shifts the thoughts and ideas the way the flow constantly stirs and shifts the sand and gravel once-mountains on their slow but constant march to the sea.

You don't stop very long in this river, just as you don't stop long in life. The flow, the sand, the spirit just won't pass you by. It erodes at your feet, burying them, uncovering them. It takes away from the support under one leg, making you move. As in life, when walking a Prairie River, you can't stop; you must move on.

Oh, you can try to remain, try to capture this spot, this place. And, for a time, you will think you've succeeded. But the river, like the flow of life, will move you.

Moving isn't easy, though. You slip and slide and sink into soft "quicksand." That isn't as bad as it sounds, just frustrating as it pulls off your boots and causes you to momentarily lose your balance. But then, life also has its small pockets of quicksand. You fall into them and, at first, it seems to be impossible to escape. But, whether walking the river or moving through the flow of life, you regain your balance, tie your bootlaces a little tighter, and move on.

Walking the river, with mountains rolling underfoot, also makes you aware of your place in all things. Another pebble, rock, simple grain of sand. Simple. An individual. Yet, a part of the complexity of an amazing whole. An important part of that whole.

There is an old argument that asks if a tree falls in the forest, and there is no one there to hear it, does the tree make a sound?

Standing here with water up to my knees, I ask: If a river moves toward the sea, with its precious cargo of mini-mountains, and no one is there to walk in it, does it flow?

You can ride a boat on the river, dam it, and swim in the momentarily distracted water. You can divert it here and there, and borrow its power and force for uses of your own, but never think you can own it, control it, stop it, or understand it.

Edward Abby once said you could gather information about something, but information isn't knowledge. And knowledge isn't understanding. To understand a river, you must not only gather information about it, gain knowledge about it, you must immerse yourself within the river, not just the water.

You must feel the flow, touch the rolling mountains underfoot, slide into the soft sand-sinks, and carry the remains on your pants to be deposited on the floor of the pickup. You must walk the river with water soaking into your boots. You must walk it, not only for yourself, and your understanding, but also, so that the river will continue to flow.

I walk this one now. Bobwhite calling from either shore. Wrens, warblers, and redwings sing. A softshell turtle slides quickly down the bank into the water. Herons squawk, and ducks panic. The flow moves around my feet as I stop to watch fish dart behind a snag in the water, a snag that proves to be the horn and skullcap of a long-dead buffalo. But I can't stay long because the river say's "move on" as it takes the sand from below my right foot. Move on!

Heraclitus, an ancient Greek philosopher who lived 500 years before Christ (535 BC - 475 BC), said you can never step twice into the same river. The river changes and always renews itself. He said, "The waters scatter and gather, come together and flow away, approach and depart." By walking in the river, you also change. Your mind shifts, and your thoughts, like the water, scatter and gather, come together and flow in ways anew so that your very being is altered with each step. Thus, we can also say that a river is never stepped into twice by the same person.

I leave the river. I move on and do what it is in life that I do. The river moves on, ever onward, doing what rivers do. But I'll return to this river, and it will be a different me, as it will be a different river. By my simple return, however, I will allow this river to do more than just move on. It will flow once again. The river, doing its part, allows my life to flow onward. Who would think the simple act of walking knee-deep in a prairie river would be that important?

www.ingramcontent.com/pod-product-compliance
Lightning Source LLC
Chambersburg PA
CBHW070550290526
45790CB00002B/628